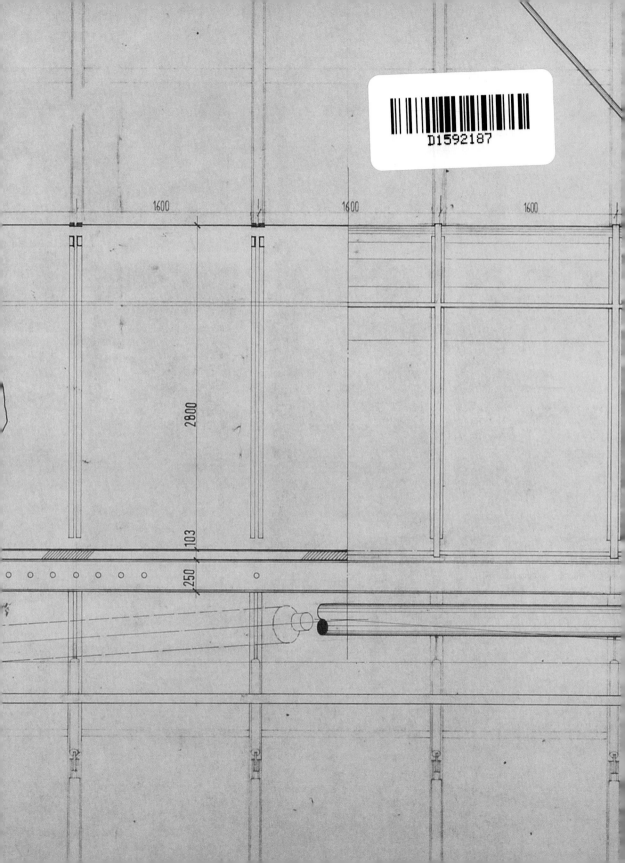

1600 1600 1600

2800

103

250

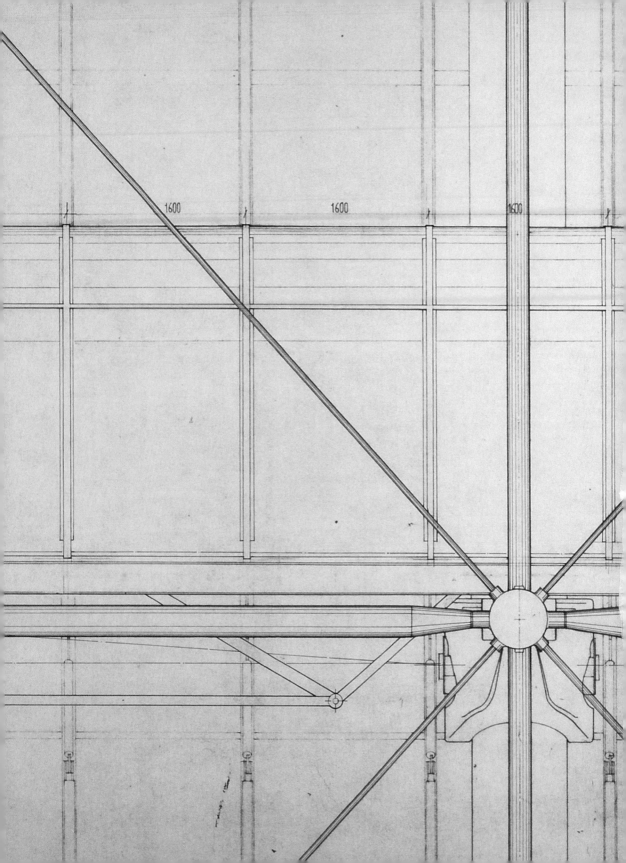

Centre Pompidou

Centre Pompidou

Renzo Piano, Richard
Rogers, and the Making
of a Modern Monument

Francesco Dal Co

Great Architects/Great Buildings

Yale University Press
New Haven and London

A short version of this essay appeared as "Beaubourg"
in Francesco Dal Co, *Renzo Piano*, published in Italian
by Electa, Milan, in 2014, and was translated into English
by Steve Piccolo.

yalebooks.com/art

This publication was assisted by the Ronald and Betty
Miller Turner Publication Fund.

Designed by Luke Bulman—Office with Camille Sacha Salvador
Typeset in Atlas Grotesk
Printed in China through Oceanic Graphic International, Inc.

Library of Congress Control Number: 2016934871
ISBN 978-0-300-22129-9

A catalogue record for this book is available from
the British Library.

This paper meets the requirements of
ANSI/NISO Z39.48-1992 (Permanence of Paper).

10 9 8 7 6 5 4 3 2 1

Cover: Facade on rue du Renard. © Michel Denancé.
Endpapers: Elevation drawing of the west facade showing the
superimposed layers of the structure. See pp. 112–13.
Frontispiece: Sequentially mounting the Warren girders, the
gerberettes, and the external tie beams. See p. 79.

Contents

Preface

In explaining how the Centre Georges Pompidou came to be designed and built, and ultimately considering how it was received and how a similar building might be seen today, I found myself in the position of having to interlace a number of different narratives, in some cases seemingly divergent. Considering the historical junctures which framed their work, I devoted particular attention to the architects' and engineers' design processes and construction choices. In order to understand what the Centre Pompidou is and what it represents, I found it necessary to examine these processes and analyze these choices along with the more complex historical circumstances behind the construction of the building.

In thinking about the many histories I was obliged to weave together, I had a sense that the numerous and varied topics covered in the book might make for fragmentary reading and that it was thus preferable to give my writing a stringent rhythm. For this reason I have, for instance, avoided including footnotes. I have instead incorporated references to the most significant literature in the text and have taken into account the personalities of the authors and topics on which they touched, allowing them to become integral parts of the story. The bibliographical note presents an overview of these sources and tries to clarify the debt I owe the authors quoted.

In the essay "How Should One Read a Book?" published in the October 1926 issue of *The Yale Review*, Virginia Woolf, who evidently thought that words carried a slightly different nature than that attributed to them by Nietzsche ("each word is a prejudice" we can read in his *Menschliches, Allzumenschliches*), argued that "words are more impalpable than bricks." She then added, though speaking of short stories and novels, that a book is always "an attempt to make something as formed and controlled as a building." Though I may slightly bend the meaning of this statement, I think that books written by those treating the history of architecture in particular should strive toward a similar goal. As for me, I have tried to follow this advice myself by giving the book the shape of an essay. The essay format allows readers and the author to enter into a "broken conversation"; but, as one of the most brilliant minds of the twentieth century, Walter

Benjamin, wrote about the Italian style of argumentation, "the 'moral' of an interrupted conversation follows after you like a lost puppy, and just when you have gone all the way there, you find yourself empty-handed" (I hope that this quotation, conveying the considerable intelligence offered in a few lines of *Über die Art der Italiener, zu diskutieren*, will not be seen as a flirtation nor be used against me).

The aim of the book, now in the hands of the reader, is not only to provide information about the construction of a building that has made its mark in recent history (and not just that of contemporary architecture). Like any book this one has the ambition to encourage those who read it to deepen their studies or to increase their curiosity, and in this way to acquire knowledge allowing them to challenge the arguments that are supported and criticized here, whether in depth or circumstantially. I think that this is the way one should interpret Virginia Woolf's exhortation to the reader, again from "How Should One Read a Book?": "Do not dictate to your author; try to become him. Be his fellow-worker and accomplice." The word that I find most important here is "fellow-worker." This compound word alludes to the fact that every book reaches its goal as soon as it encourages the reader to "work together" on the topic that the book has brought to his or her attention, as the word "accomplice" suggests with a certain wanted emphasis.

For those who desire to take this advice and deepen their knowledge of the history of the Centre Georges Pompidou—or the histories that Centre Pompidou inspired— there is no lack of tools. The literature dedicated to this work, familiar to many as simply "Beaubourg," is vast, and heterogeneous at that. In the bibliographical note at the end of this book, I have tried to tell readers how it served me, and rather than merely presenting a list of titles, I have offered explanation of how and to what extent I have acted as a "fellow-worker" toward their authors.

The variety and breadth of literature that is related to the Centre Georges Pompidou, either directly or indirectly, confirms that it is often more complicated for a historian to deal with a topic close at hand than from a distance. The passing of time helps to select sources, and it narrows down the number of documents and puts them into perspective, which is not to say that it puts them in the "right" perspective. Putting the facts in the "right" perspective is not time's concern—that is up to the historian. But it is no longer acceptable to think that the historian's job is to represent the past "wie es eigentlich gewesen" (as it actually happened), as the nineteenth-century German historian Leopold von Ranke thought. Indeed, formulating this precept "father" Ranke provided "a powerful narcotic to the nineteenth century," as Benjamin subsequently asserted, some effects of which still linger today. Therefore the perspective in which the historian places the historical facts can never be the "right" one. To grapple with historical events implies the need to choose and decide, with the understanding that every choice and each decision can never be objective. What's more, the words "decision" and "choice" imply etymologically the necessity to abbreviate, as happens often in the genre of essay writing on which I have relied (*decidere* in Latin is formed from *de*, implying a removal, and *caedere*, which means to cut).

When one treats a contemporary topic, however, the sources and documents accumulate and multiply in an erratic fashion, which creates additional difficulties for interpreting them and for making choices and decisions wisely. Things become still more complicated when the historian writes about events with which he has coexisted. To be a contemporary of that which you treat is not necessarily an advantage. Proximity in time, and the closer the more problematic, can result in a distorted observation of events, similar to that suffered with conditions of vision such as diplopia, or double vision. One effect of this condition is a difficulty in separating the abundance of readily available information because of the different ways in which this same information is represented. This difficulty is inherent in the conditions of closeness and proximity in which this book took shape.

In addition, to be a contemporary or even a participant in the events that you want to interpret makes it complicated to study them without becoming victim to that which often accompanies factual evidence, the "invented tradition." I employ here, with a small stretch, terminology from *The Invention of Tradition* by Eric Hobsbawm and Terence Ranger (1983). "Invented traditions" also include those "emerging in a less easily traceable manner within a brief and datable period . . . and establishing themselves with great rapidity," wrote Hobsbawm, citing as a rather prosaic example to communicate to his readers the wide spectrum of the meanings of this concept "the appearance and development of the practices associated with the Cup Final in British Association Football."

In writing about the Centre Georges Pompidou and studying its history, I think it necessary and not just opportune to grapple with the invention of a tradition. This tradition, nourished by legends of various origins, has contributed not only to the building's extraordinary success but also to an obfuscation of its real nature. The same tradition has transformed Centre Pompidou into a gathering place for rituals accompanying the formation of beliefs, as well as the styles and tastes of contemporary life, the continuous development of what Elias Canetti, in his extraordinary book *Crowds and Power* (1960), had called the "drive of the masses." If I may say so, liberating Beaubourg from this invented tradition was one of my goals in writing this book.

Chapter One
Paris 1968: "Reform Yes, Masquerade No"

On May 29, 1968, the French prime minister Georges Pompidou was in Paris, but he did not know—so the story goes—where the president of the Fifth Republic was at the time. General Charles de Gaulle, president since 1959, had left the city without informing even his closest aides.

Two months prior, on March 22, students had protested the Vietnam War and the reforms known as the Fouchet plan by occupying the literature department at the University of Paris in Nanterre. Named after Christian Fouchet, minister of national education from 1962 to 1967, the plan's educational component was intended to prepare growing numbers of students to meet the needs of modern industrial technocracy. During the protests several students were detained and faced expulsion, and on May 2 the administration shut down the university at Nanterre. That day students in Paris occupied the Sorbonne in solidarity with the Nanterre students, and on May 3 the Sorbonne was invaded by police. Four days later, 50,000 students marched through Paris's Latin Quarter to protest police brutality; three days after that, the streets of the quarter were barricaded. The student upheaval quickly joined with growing tensions among the working class, and on May 13 a general strike involving over ten million workers paralyzed Paris and other regions of France, and, in a formidable demonstration of solidarity, the students and workers marched through the streets of Paris. On May 25 and 26, at the Ministry of Labor on rue de Grenelle in Paris, government representatives headed by Georges Pompidou, unions, and business organizations conducted long, difficult negotiations (managed by the young secretary of state Jacques Chirac, who would become mayor of Paris in 1977 and later president of the republic in 1995). On May 27 their agreement, though reached with much difficulty, and which would have guaranteed an increase in salaries and the minimum wage (SMIG), was rejected by the workers.

Two days later, on May 29, de Gaulle, traveling incognito, left Paris for Baden Baden, where he met with the French military

Demonstration in Paris, May 1968. Protesters with a banner against Georges Pompidou and Pierre Messmer, minister of armies, 1960–66.

command in Germany (created after the end of World War II in 1945). The commander of the contingent was General Jacques Massu, who in 1940 while stationed in Africa had responded, as had Fouchet, to the appeal for resistance against the German occupation of France launched by General de Gaulle from London on June 18, 1940. Later Massu fought in Indochina and on the banks of the Suez Canal when, in 1956, President Gamal Abdel Nasser of Egypt nationalized the Compagnie Universelle du Canal Maritime de Suez, which since 1858 had been French and English property. In 1957 Massu and the Tenth Parachute Division he headed temporarily squelched the anti-French revolt guided by Algeria's National Liberation Front, winning the Battle of Algiers, as these events became known following the magnificent movie of 1966 *La Battaglia di Algeri* by Gillo Pontecorvo.

De Gaulle, after meeting with Massu in Baden Baden and sure of his support, headed back to Paris. On May 19, a few days after negotiations had started at rue de Grenelle, at the end of a cabinet meeting Georges Pompidou summed up the general's guidelines for his ministers: "La réforme oui, la chienlit non." *Chienlit*, an archaic term also used by François Rabelais in the sixteenth century, can be translated in a variety of ways: masquerade or pantomime, but also mess, chaos, disgrace, public disorder (*pagaille*), and de Gaulle may also have had in mind the meaning familiar in the soldierly jargon he knew well, "chie-en-lit" (shit in bed). Setting aside that possible implied overtone of the word, the masculine noun *chienlit*, in its original version, *chien-en-lit*, was also the name of a Parisian carnival mask. For this reason we imagine that Georges Gorse, at the time minister of information, and Georges Pompidou spoke the word *chienlit*—we'll meet it again in the following pages—to the French television interviewers in the spirit of its original context of referring to people marching in the Paris boulevards: a person who walks the street in a mask or dressed in a bizarre costume. For the purposes of these pages it is more appropriate to assume that the phrase's translation is "Reform yes, masquerade no," which in any case derives from de Gaulle's conviction that what was happening in Paris was an unacceptable carnival, a revival of the time when any rule can be transgressed by anybody protected by a mask. This intention of the French government and the unusual intransigence of the May 1968 happenings in the streets of Paris and through French society was not only treated with irony, but this incisive,

explicit watchword would backfire on de Gaulle, who made his definitive exit from political life less than one year later.

On April 28, 1969, de Gaulle announced his resignation. On June 15, Georges Pompidou succeeded him as head of state. A few months later, at the end of 1969, Pompidou approved the general program for the construction of an unusual cultural center located near Les Halles. He was at the start of his term, and the walls of Paris still bore visible signs of the posters that students had hung there just over a year earlier, screen-printed by the Atelier Populaire that took form in May 1968 at the École des Beaux-Arts. From 1969 until his death in 1974, Pompidou promoted governmental action that focused on the development of high-tech industry and a new energy policy, undertook profound transformations of infrastructures, and offered incisive urban planning projects. Even before the 1973 energy crisis, he had created a new Ministry of the Environment and revitalized the role of the state as a promoter of cultural life. The memory of the man and his work is now embodied in the building that bears his name.

The construction of the Centre Pompidou cannot be explained, nor can the meaning of the building be adequately understood, without taking into account the events of 1968 and the perspective they give us on aspects of French cultural and political life. In addition to these themes, to which we will return, certain other factors deserve our attention.

When, at the end of 1969, Pompidou announced his intention to build a cultural center of unprecedented character and size in Paris, his goals were quite clear. Speaking in private about General de Gaulle, he observed: "What a great pity that such a great man did not leave behind him a monument." Unlike his predecessor, who had different political priorities and believed he had been given other tasks, Pompidou saw the necessity of reasserting France's role on the political and economic world stage and in particular in the sphere of culture, at the same time restoring the eminence of a president's own initiatives. For reasons similar to those that had prompted André Malraux—a key cultural figure during the first half of the twentieth century and France's minister of culture from 1959 to 1969—to think about building a large museum of the twentieth century in the capital in the 1970s, Pompidou hoped to give a positive boost to Paris. This point of view was particularly apt given the city's competition with New York in an era in which—as French historian

Marc Fumaroli coquettishly wrote in *Paris–New York et retour* (2009)—not only in the world of art "the old aristocratic game of tastes had given way to the game of supply and demand, to its roulette and relative combinations." Such words capture an aspect of Pompidou's political strategy, that of ensuring the autonomy of France from the ruling role of the United States while ensuring for France leadership in Europe.

No matter the vantage point, one cannot help but suppose that Pompidou's decision was also a consequence of a certain event of May 1968, one that had had a strong impact on international public opinion, revealing the feverish tone that had infected Paris during the more intense weeks of protest. On the night of May 15, protesters had occupied the Théâtre de l'Odéon and the Place de l'Odéon. Actors, directors, workers, and the general public were involved in the gatherings and meetings. One of the leading institutions of French culture, the theater had been opened in 1782 by Marie Antoinette to host the Comédie-Française. When the protestors proclaimed it the "ex-Théâtre de France," this was an event with symbolic impact, transforming one of the most prestigious French cultural institutions into a space whose temporary and permanent inhabitants were engaged, as they proclaimed, in a "work of reflection on our rejection of the spectacle as merchandise and on the possibility that has now been opened up to give life to an art of struggle."

Pompidou was a man of culture, and his wife, Claude Cahour, possessed a lively intellect and was well informed about current cultural trends. She was to play an important role in the creation of the institution that would later bear her husband's name. These circumstances also help explain how it came about that a parcel of land was set aside for the new cultural center in a place that was endowed with a symbolic value as lofty as that of the Odéon. Moreover, Pompidou was aware that the redevelopment of this area—earmarked already in 1968 to be the site of the new Bibliothèque des Halles to respond to the needs of the Bibliothèque Nationale—would mean promoting reform in the center of Paris, renewing its status as the capital of *embellissement stratégique* (strategic beautification), to borrow the name of the committee that Napoleon III had created in 1853, the Commission des Embellissements de Paris, and under which Georges Eugène Haussmann, prefect of the Seine from 1853 to 1870, had addressed the network of Parisian urban, administrative, and economic reforms. Thinking

Paris, Halles Centrales, the new central markets, exterior view of the pavilions, from *L'Illustration*, 1857.

to intervene on Plateau Beaubourg between the Halles and
Marais districts, Pompidou and his advisors in fact strove to
bring to completion a process of urban reform: the renovation
of an ailing patch of the city that had been slated for renewal
since the 1930s and had been addressed in studies by Le
Corbusier that were never implemented. They hoped to bring
about a turning point in the debate triggered by the 1965 decision to move the most important market in Paris, Les Halles,
to Rungis on the outskirts of the city. Four years later, in 1969,
the characteristic pavilions of the central market of Paris were
abandoned. (Almost immediately, though, they were repur-
posed to host a range of cultural initiatives, entering a new
life that in spite of its brief span—from March 1969 to October
1970—gained enough popularity to leave many regrets in Paris
as well as among the international intellectual community.)

Halfway through the nineteenth century, the construction of Les Halles—designed by Victor Baltard and Félix
Emmanuel Callet, a work destined to meet with universal
acclaim—had been the cause of one of the fiercest battles
between the different strategies of Napoleon III's renovation
program. Baltard had managed to overcome an arduous con-
frontation with several architects (among them Hector Horeau),
the emperor's hesitations, and Haussmann's opposition to his
previous proposals, demonstrating that "the spirit of lightness
and economy" of his latest project for the market responded "to
every point of view of the new administration's expectations."
In 1853, to demonstrate the quality of his proposal, Baltard

GRAND COMBLE

Coupe suivant l'axe
de l'un des Grands Pavillons.

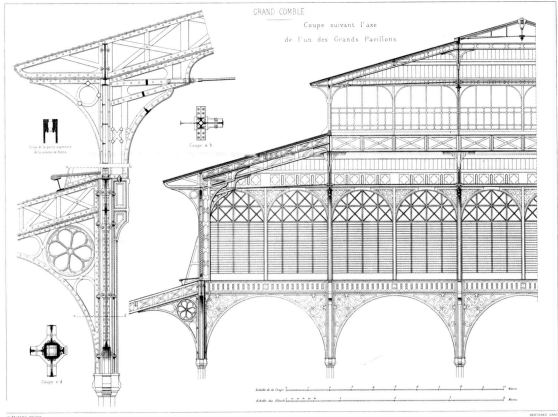

Coupe de la partie supérieure
de la colonne en fonte

Coupe a b

Coupe c d

Echelle de la Coupe

Echelle des Détails

V. BALTARD ARCH.TE

BERTRAND GRAV.T

GRANDS PAVILLONS ___ DÉTAILS DES COMBLES

COMBLE SUPERIEUR

Projections des fermes d'arêtier
du troisième Comble

Projections des fermes droites
du troisième Comble

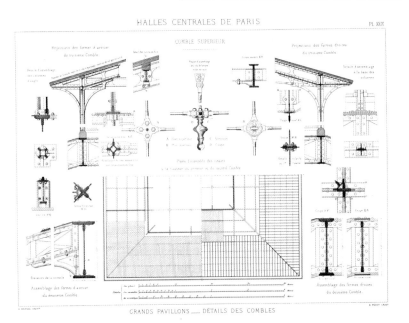

Détail d'assemblage
des colonnes
d'angle

Détail d'assemblage
à la base des
colonnes

Plans d'ensemble des droits
à la hauteur du premier et du second Comble

Assemblage des fermes d'arêtier
du deuxième Comble

Assemblage des fermes droites
du deuxième Comble

GRANDS PAVILLONS ___ DÉTAILS DES COMBLES

called into play a "spirit" that was the expression of values such as "lightness and economy." A century later, this very same spirit would be not just evoked but implemented when Renzo Piano, Richard Rogers, Gianni Franchini, and Ove Arup & Partners presented their project for Plateau Beaubourg.

The correspondence is neither strange nor by chance. Baltard and Callet's project and their building—the great achievement of Pierre-François Joly, the *forgeon serrurier* (blacksmith) who created, along with his son-in-law César Jolly who did the load calculations, the metal structures—provided an unmistakable epochal breakthrough of progress in the history of architecture. Although controversial, it was perceived differently at different times through the intervening century. As Alfred Gotthold Meyer explained in *Eisenbauten* (1907), the pavilions of Les Halles were light and economical thanks to the "victory" of the principle and the technical implications of tectonics (iron) over those of stereotomy (stone). Meyer's book truly "never ceases to surprise," as Walter Benjamin marveled: in its description of architecture's selective evolution in the nineteenth century leading to the rise of tectonics over stereotomy, it suggests or even precisely identifies one of the main reasons why, about sixty years later, the project by Piano, Rogers, and their team gained favor in the competition to redevelop Plateau Beaubourg. If "the first constructions in iron served transitory purposes," as Benjamin observed in his masterful *Arcades Project* (1927–1940, unfinished), the Centre Pompidou sealed the transformation of the functional and transitory into the formal and the stable.

Furthermore, the construction by Piano, Rogers, Franchini, and the Ove Arup & Partners engineers, again to quote Meyer, satisfies "the need for large, undivided spaces," determined by their roofs, where "the lateral walls are 'hidden,' so to speak." From this building, we might add, the *chienlit*, the masquerade, has been banned, as the accomplished twentieth-century architect Carlo Scarpa commented on the view of the elevation of the Centre Pompidou visible from rue de Temple. Scarpa's cultural attitude toward architecture was evidently different from that of Piano and Rogers, but what he admired in their building was the fact that the rear facade, "hidden" as it is, was given form by the building's "tools"—the technical, functional elements used by the architects and the engineers to control the circulation of what is light and mostly invisible in a building, the fluids, and what

9   **Paris 1968**

is dynamic, the vertical movements—which have been transformed into parts of a formal composition. For these reasons and having in mind the pages of Meyer and Benjamin just quoted, it is not surprising that, from its first appearance as a design, the building on Plateau Beaubourg has been seen in relation to the Eiffel Tower. The construction of that tower during the second half of nineteenth century marked the triumph of the "minimum dimension, the first phenomenological form of the principle of assembly" (Benjamin). As a careful reader of the influential Swiss architectural historian Sigfried Giedion's Bauen in Frankreich, Bauen in Eisen, Bauen in Eisenbeton (Building in France, Building in Iron, Building in Ferroconcrete), published in 1928, Benjamin understood the importance for contemporary architecture of the principle of weight reduction of the components and of transformation of the building in a process of assembly, the very same strategy adopted by Joly for the building of the Halles that was destined to be developed and applied in the Centre Pompidou.

In a letter of December 1969, Pompidou informed Malraux's successor as minister of culture, Edmond Michelet (who also had been a member of the French Resistance during the German Occupation), that he had decided on the purpose of the vast Plateau Beaubourg and planned to hold a competition to choose the designers of a new cultural center. In 1971, despite a heated movement to conserve the old Halles, the Parisian municipal administration issued the permit to demolish the market pavilions to allow the construction of an underground station of the regional rail system (RER). Yet the administration had not made final decisions about how the land once occupied by the pavilions would be used. As complaints and quarrels flew between municipal and national administrations, there began a flowering of projects, proposals, and statements, from architects and cultural figures of all orders and ranks, offering solutions for what to construct in place of the beloved Halles. Protestors and some of the media decried Pompidou's proposal for the cultural center as an unacceptable reparation for destroying Les Halles, a magnificent building considered a monument and a landmark of the "unchangeable beauty of Paris," a commonplace consistently repeated since the nineteenth century by the French intelligentsia. But ironically the connection between the destruction of Les Halles and the construction of Centre Pompidou includes an unnoticed paradox, as Les Halles had

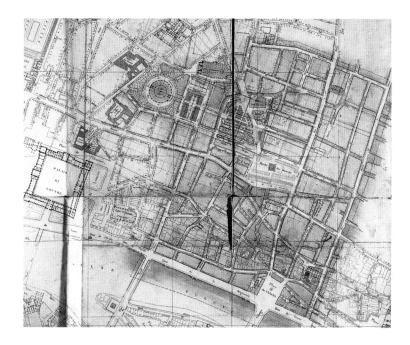

Map of the Halles district, c. 1860.

been the consequence of the deepest and most radical urban transformation, orchestrated by Haussmann, that Paris had suffered in its entire history, the most clear demonstration also that Paris's beauty is the byproduct of continuous "changes."

This situation created a historical distortion that left the fate of the venerable steel-and-glass structure by Baltard, Callet, and Joly firmly and perhaps inevitably associated with that of Plateau Beaubourg: even after the Centre Pompidou's opening, its lukewarm reception, in often misleading and unjustified ways, was influenced by the collective resentment of those who had lost the "battle" to save the noble century-old pavilions of the Paris central market.

In 1969, however, Pompidou had no adversaries capable of challenging him, and he had a clarity of purpose developed out of the painful experiences as de Gaulle's prime minister in 1968 and the legacy of Malraux. Pompidou held a high opinion of his role and the need to shape the modes by which his political function was represented. Wanting to give Paris a new cultural center while redeveloping its "heart," as he put it, the French president cast himself as the unchallenged orchestrator.

Pompidou decided that the design competition for the new construction would be open to any architect in the world, and (echoing a lesson learned from May 1968) no matter if the winner "serait-il jeune et dépourvu de moyens financiers" (might be young and without a solid financial position)—a condition the French president could not have known Piano and Rogers, in their thirties in 1971, would genuinely match. This open and tolerant approach, however, did not imply an abdication of the decision-making power of Pompidou himself. In fact, as the competition guidelines made clear, there was no promise that the winner selected by the jury would actually be commissioned to design what Pompidou imagined as an "architectural and urban ensemble that represents our time"—and this condition throws particular light on the results of the competition.

View of the Plateau Beaubourg and Les Halles, c. 1960.

The president created an organizational structure that was not only independent on an administrative level but, even more significantly, independent of the Ministry of Culture. He made use of a group of officials of proven experience from public administration and not necessarily connected with the ministry. Their activities were guided by Sébastien Loste, a connoisseur of, among other things, the history of the Universal Expositions, while the preparation of the program was assigned to the young architect François Lombard and involved experts such as François Barré, later president of the Centre Pompidou (1993–96), Germain Viatte, former member of the Direction des Musées de France, and the librarian Bernard Schulz. Finally, the president assigned the role of supervisor in charge of the project's implementation to a proven state advisor, Robert Bordaz, who, although as a man in his sixties did not have that trait of youthfulness so appreciated by Pompidou, could nevertheless bring great experience as an administrator. Bordaz indeed had developed his experience in a range of state initiatives after having directed the cabinet of Eugène Claudius-Petit, one of the most important and distinctive figures of post-war France as minister of reconstruction. Without Bordaz—"a genius," according to Piano—"nothing would have happened," declared Peter Rice, the engineer who collaborated with Piano, Rogers, and Franchini on their submission and later had a pivotal role in the construction of Beaubourg.

The guidelines created by Pompidou's organization were simple. They exemplified the "Cartesian clarity of French administrative praxis," in Rice's words. Besides the detailed recommendations, to which we will return, in substance the guidelines asked the participants to design, on an area of 5 acres (2 hectares), a building of over a million square feet (96,000 square meters) whose goal was to give a roof not to

a new museum but to a multifaceted complex of cultural functions. As we will see, it may be a bit misleading or excessive to consider this program—which Marc Fumaroli did in *L'État culturel* (1991), one of his more polemical but enlightening books on French cultural politics—as the origin of a new "permanent Universal Exposition of art and technology." But before returning to this topic and discussion of the meaning of Centre Pompidou, it is time to address our attention to the way in which Beaubourg was conceived and designed.

Chapter Two
Butterfly Effects: Beaubourg's Architects and Engineers

At the start of 1971, the competition announcement for Paris's new cultural center reached the desk of engineer Edmund "Ted" Happold in London, and he decided to spend the two hundred francs required by the organizers to take part in the competition and receive the guidelines. Happold was at the helm of Structure 3, one of the structural design departments created after 1967 in the office of the consulting engineering studio Ove Arup & Partners, where Peter Rice was also working. Founded in 1946 and shaped by the experiences of its founder, Ove Arup, this company was a leading engineering office in the 1960s and 1970s and today has about a hundred branches around the world. Arup was born in Newcastle, England, and studied first philosophy then engineering at Copenhagen University and the Technical University of Denmark, concluding his studies in 1922. During the 1930s he worked in England with the most respectable English architects associated with the Modern Architectural Research Group (MARS), of which he was a member, the London-based branch of the International Congresses of Modern Architecture (CIAM), and in particular with the leading exponent of this association, Berthold Lubetkin, the Russian architect born in Tbilisi who had a critical role

Members of the Piano & Rogers studio at the excavation of Centre Beaubourg, 1972. To the left, one member of the studio salutes the photographer with a clenched fist.

Renzo Piano, Su Rogers, Richard Rogers, Ted Happold, and Peter Rice in front of a presentation board featuring their design for the Centre Beaubourg competition, Paris, 1971.

in the development of the modern architectural culture in England during the 1930s and 1940s. Happold joined the Arup studio in 1957, after completing his university studies. Later he spent two years in the United States, working for the Norwegian-born engineer Fred Severud, then associated with the construction of the St. Louis Gateway Arch (designed in 1948 but completed in 1965 by Eero Saarinen, who has a minor but unexpected role in our story, as we will see).

In 1967 Ove Arup & Partners enjoyed broad renown and could count on excellent commissions. Povl Ahm, a Danish-born engineer, was the partner in charge of Structure 3 for the firm; he had already contributed to the construction of the podium for the Sydney Opera House in Australia, collaborating with Jørn Utzon, winner of the 1956 design competition, an undertaking to which the Australian government assigned the utmost importance. In 1967 the development of the project for the Mecca Conference Center in Saudi Arabia prompted Structure 3 to establish a close relationship with the German architect Frei Otto, who started his professional activity in Berlin in 1952 and was creator of the Federal Republic of Germany's pavilion at Expo 67 in Montreal. After their initial meeting in 1967 at Riyadh, Otto and Happold formed a friendship that included other designers from Structure 3 and was reinforced in the following years.

The projects later developed by Structure 3 with Otto were numerous and at times emblematically spectacular, as in the case of the 1971 Arctic City plan, whose preparation also involved, among others, the famous Japanese architect Kenzo Tange, whom Rice admired greatly. These works are a consequence of the interest raised by the first achievements of Otto, to whom contemporary architectural culture owes an enormous debt for his experiments and research in the field of tensostructures, thin vaults, and light roofing systems. The temporary pavilions he constructed for the Bundesgartenschau in Kassel in 1955 and at the Interbau 1957 in Berlin were widely known and were studied not least by the young engineers working at Ove Arup & Partners. In 1964, at the urging of Fritz Leonhardt, one of the great structural engineers of the twentieth century, Otto founded the Institute for the Study of Light Structures at the University of Stuttgart; the research center that took form there quickly became a point of reference for designers like those gathered in Structure 3 and for Renzo Piano and Richard Rogers.

From the beginning of Piano's career, his works reveal his interest in and admiration for Otto's buildings and research. From the middle of the 1960s until the end of the 1980s, Piano's works not only show the influence of Otto but also reveal a designer capable of turning out a stream of experiments with construction techniques to permit light roofs and enclosures under tension: the Pavilion of Italian Industry for the Expo '70 in Osaka, Japan; the Urban Regeneration Workshop for UNESCO in Otranto, Italy, ten years later; the tensostructure located in the garden facing the Schlumberger factory in Paris (1981–84); and, above all, two paradigms of quality and elegance for their construction details—the IBM Traveling Pavilion (1983), created with Peter Rice and formed by thirty-four isostatic three-hinged arches with a reticular structure, and the offices for the Lowara factory at Montecchio Maggiore near Vicenza, Italy (1984–85).

Furthermore, Otto's experiments matched the line of inquiry that the American Buckminster Fuller had opened in the 1920s with his project for the Dymaxion house, which later, mainly during Fuller's stay at Black Mountain College in North Carolina in 1948–49, developed into experiments with geodesic domes. The German architect admired Fuller even if he did not share his prophetic tone; Otto acknowledged the parallels between his work and the system of construction the American inventor was testing that would allow a building to span a large amount of space with a minimum construction weight. In 1971, the same year as the Beaubourg competition, Otto presented the already mentioned City in the Arctic project, sponsored by Farbwerke Hoechst AG, which he conceived along with Kenzo Tange + URTEC and Arup's Structures 3, which included both Happold and Rice. The project proposed a shallow dome with a span of about 6,500 feet (1,981 meters), supported by the pressure of the interior air, exploiting a principle critically different from the one for a transparent geodesic dome over Manhattan that had been conceived around 1960 by Fuller with the collaboration of Shoji Sadao. But in spite of their differences, and having in mind that Otto developed his first studies for large-span urban roofs at the beginning of the 1950s, it is clear that the German architect and the American inventor were moving on paths leading in the same direction. And, even if not completely accurate, this was certainly the general perception during the 1960s, notably after 1967 when Fuller built the United States pavilion at Expo 67 in Montreal,

Architectural Design, March 1971, cover and page 144 with the article "Lennart Grut, Ted Happold, and Peter Rice Discuss Frei Otto and His Work."

Renzo Piano, District Workshop for UNESCO at Otranto, Italy, 1969; prospectus and built laboratory photographed during a meeting with Piano.

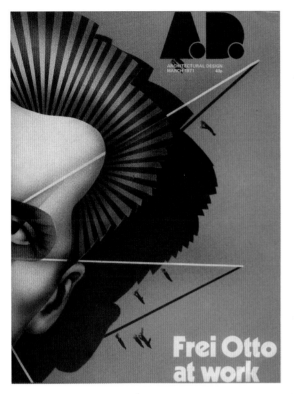

A.D.
ARCHITECTURAL DESIGN
MARCH 1971   40p

Frei Otto
at work

Lennart Grut (L) Ted Happold (T) and Peter Rice (P) discuss Frei Otto and his work

They felt that their differing attitudes towards Frei and his relationship with them could best be explained in dialogue. This would illustrate how they saw him, what he is like to work with and what they learned from him – not criticizing him but hoping to help understand him.

T The problem in talking about Frei Otto is that we are all engineers and this conditions how we see him and what he shows of himself to us.
P He certainly finds engineers very difficult because they are always restrictive. His biggest problem is that engineers are a restricting and restraining force in his life and they are continually containing him. On the other hand, there is nothing he enjoys more than to be well thought of by engineers.
L Peter has known Frei for two and a half years and I for only two, but you, Ted, have known him for longer.
T I first met Frei Otto after the UIA limited competition for the Conference Centres for Riyadh and Mecca which was held in 1966. We were in partnership with Trevor Dannatt and he was asked to carry out the Centre for Riyadh and Frei Otto and Rolf Gutbrod were asked to design the Centre for Mecca. I knew Frei Otto's work of course and when he and Rolf Gutbrod asked us to be their engineers we

were very pleased. They were both entailed in the construction of the Federal Pavilion for Montreal at the time so I can include some of that in my first hand experience of him, but I have only personally known him since that time and there is a tremendous volume of his work I know little about.
Between the three of us we have controlled all the detail work our practice has done with Frei, but we certainly could not be definitive about him.
L The problem in trying to define the way he works and the skills he brings to a design team for me is that I am trying to comment on him from very specific meetings and this is very difficult. Perhaps we should begin by discussing some of his background.
T Both his father and grandfather were sculptors and woodcarvers. He was a pilot during the Second World War though still very young. When he was captured he was put in a prisoner of war camp near Chartres and, while there, was engaged on rebuilding work. Then he went to university, took a degree in architecture, and his famous books were his doctoral theses. I think life in Germany as a student was quite a struggle then.
L What about his practical work? Is one of the sides of the way he works and the type of person he is, that he has never worked in a practical sense as part of a design team? He seems to me to have always worked with ideas.
T I think he understands the

problem of a design team. When we started work with Rolf Gutbrod and Frei on the Mecca project, we were moving into a field we had not worked in before and, as the programme was tight, I felt strongly that if we could separate the engineering problems into separate sections it would be feasible to build up a group with expertise. So we agreed to separate the roof of the main auditorium from the main structure and to seal the building with unloaded links in order to isolate the main roof's engineering problems. Frei accepted our problem, even though he did not believe the roof was difficult to analyse or define. You know how difficult we found it to discover who, among our engineers, were able to work in this field and I think Frei showed great patience with our learning.
P In spite of the fact that I agree with all the reasons why you felt it necessary to do so, I think it was a flaw to separate the roof from the structure. The point is a measure of Frei's commitment to architecture.
T To continue the point. He has worked a lot with manufacturers. Peter Stromeyer, the famous tent maker, financed him for a long time and he designed the majority of the tents in the Stromeyer catalogue – at least the big ones. I think the first cables used to reinforce tents were the ones he was consultant for at the Swiss National Exhibition in Lausanne. He had done a similar

shaped one for a garden exhibition but I don't think that had cables. So prior to Lausanne he was using membranes. For the Lausanne ones cable nets were sewn into the canvas, with plastic sleeves, and there was a difference in behaviour between the cables and the canvas – not bad but enough to be noticeable.

Interior, Lausanne cable net.

Lausanne, cable sleeve detail.

T I think this led to the solution of separating the cable net from the membrane at Montreal. The reason the separation was quite a large one was because the accuracy of measuring the cables and the membranes was not close enough and the behaviour was relatively incompatible.
P There is an interesting difference here. A membrane is not a shear free surface, whereas a cable net is. The difference between the two is that he can do with cables things he could never do with his membranes without a great deal of work. I do not believe, in strict terms anyway, that the Montreal structure would have existed if he had tried to do it from the first as a membrane.
P In thinking of Frei it is important to appreciate the fact that he has created modelling techniques which take him all the way from the initial concept of the design to the final structure. This integrated use of models, both as an inventive design and finally an analysis tool, is very unusual and may be unique. The whole process is geared at each stage to solving the problem being tackled in a positive manner.

150b

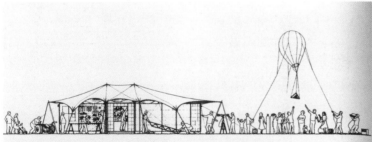

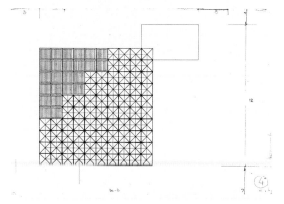

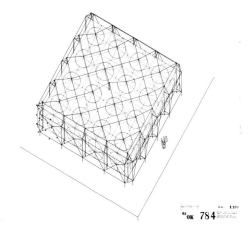

Renzo Piano, Studio Piano, Genoa, 1968–69; plan of the roof and views of the exterior and interior.

sharing the stage with Otto and his West German pavilion. While Otto's pavilion was a tensile steel cable-net structure, the Fuller construction was a spectacular example of "tensegrity" (tensile integrity), as he defined it, a construction in which the parts under tension are continuous, and those in compression are isolated, thus resembling what he called "islands in a sea of tensions." The 1967 United States pavilion further boosted Fuller's fame. Though it might be taken for granted, this success also increased the attention the young and more inquiring architects and engineers around the world gave to his "preaching," and above all to his challenge to architects to venture into "outlaw areas," uncharted territories not connected with traditional practices and disciplines, where according to Fuller "the whole development of technology has been."

In the 1960s many architects believed the time was ripe to begin to "range far from lands ruled by laws," as Fuller recommended, and to follow his "transgressive proposals," as Piano put it, with the aim of setting architecture back in step with contemporary developments of technique and technology. If "Mies tries to confuse me saying 'less is more'"—said Fuller, colorfully applying the popular slogan formulated by Mies van der Rohe precisely for the architectural culture of the "first machine age"—we need to be aware that "that's hardly the same as doing more with less in making an airplane."

Philip Johnson, one of the influential architects of the twentieth century, called Fuller "inventor, guru, and poet." But the reasons behind the success of Fuller's works and writings, and their appeal for young designers on both sides of the Atlantic, are better summed up by what Reyner Banham wrote in his seminal book *Theory and Design in the First Machine Age* (1960). After having studied at the Courtauld Institute of Art in London under Anthony Blunt, Sigfried Giedion, and Nikolaus Pevsner, when Banham published *Theory and Design in the First Machine Age* he provided an influential tool for the critical understanding of the whole culture of architecture in the twentieth century, and at the end of the book, disclosing a belief destined to become popular through the 1960s, he defined Fuller as the precursor of a new era for architecture charged with, in the inventor's own words, reconciling the "unstoppable wave of change with continuous acceleration that governs the world of technology." Banham spoke of Fuller even more eloquently as a reincarnation of the Italian architect Antonio Sant'Elia, author of the drawings called

Renzo Piano, Italian Industry Pavilion, Expo '70, Osaka, Japan; axonometric plan and detail of revetment.

Buckminster Fuller with students at Black Mountain College, near Asheville, North Carolina, 1949.

La città nuova (1914), the architectural "manifesto" of the Futurism movement. Banham's paratactic utterance of the alternatives he thought contemporary architects were facing with which he concluded his book should come as no surprise. We read on the last page of *Theory and Design in the First Machine Age*:

> The architect who proposes to run with technology knows now that he will be in fast company, and that, in order to keep up, he may have to emulate the Futurists and discard his whole cultural load, including the professional garments by which he is recognized as an architect. If, on the other hand, he decides not to do this, he may find that a technological culture has decided to go on without him. It is a choice that the masters of the Twenties failed to observe until they had made it by accident, but it is the kind of accident that architecture may not survive a second time.

Buckminster Fuller inside a model of the United States Pavilion's geodesic dome at Expo 67, Montreal, 1967.

Buckminster Fuller and Shoji Sadao, Dome over Manhattan, c. 1960.

Testifying to Banham's intelligence and foresight, this is the course that Piano, Rogers, Franchini, and the engineers from Ove Arup & Partners would follow in the construction of the Centre Pompidou eleven years later.

If all this explains why Piano and Rogers list Fuller among their masters, what we have said about Otto helps us understand his role—though a marginal, indirect one—in advising Happold for the Plateau Beaubourg competition. The aspect of Otto's work that influenced the young engineers of Structure 3 in the Ove Arup & Partners office was summed up by Rice in a conversation with Happold and Lennart Grut, all three of whom were working on the development of the project for Plateau Beaubourg. The transcription of this conversation was published in March 1971 in *Architectural Design*, at the time the unchallenged point of reference for open-minded international architectural thought. The issue of the English magazine was devoted to Otto, and among the various opinions expressed by the three authors, those of Rice deserve particular attention because they emphasize Otto's working method, novelty, and the pivotal role he assigned to the building of three-dimensional structural models in his creative process. "This integrated use of models," Rice said, "both as an inventive design and finally an analysis tool, is very unusual and may be unique. The whole process is geared at each stage to solving the problem being tackled in a positive manner."

When the issue of *Architectural Design* was published, Piano and Rice had already become friends, and the former had been developing a design strategy similar to Otto's. As he would continue to do throughout the course of his career, Piano was already using models in the way Rice attributes to Otto, as tools making it possible to "see" the forces at work in a building by observing the deformations of materials subjected to loads and identifying the most appropriate ways to counter them. These observations enabled the designers to penetrate form and structure to make compositional and construction decisions that guaranteed the most efficient distribution of stresses. In addition to models for studying the plastic configurations of nodes in three dimensions, Piano used drawings and sketches in a personal and logical manner. As is evident from his published sketches, his graphic working notes are synthetically precise and expressive, recalling a cartographer's in the way they establish in two dimensions lines corresponding to the locations of forces and tensions, from which to grasp the forms diagrammatically. Regarding these two modes of investigation, the manual construction of models, which Piano had cultivated since the start of his career, can be contrasted with the sketch method, which has something in common with carving. Piano's work comes from a continuous intertwining of static conceptions from which he draws his precise language. Carving—the tracing left on paper—and modeling—defining forms shaped by forces—both lie at the origin of the architectural work. Pavel Florensky, instructor in the most important Russian school of architecture, the Vkhutemas, in 1923 and 1924 had written about carving and modeling, that they both imply subtraction, the reduction of the material, the limitation of weight, and lightness.

"You have to have lightness inside you, because it is not just a physical thing, it is a mental thing," Piano has claimed. And his words explain something about his sketches, containing an echo of what he had learned over the course of his heterodox background—he frequented the construction sites supervised by his father (instead of university lecture halls), worked in the studio of Franco Albini in Milan, and gained a curiosity that led him to attend Jean Prouvé's courses at the Conservatoire National des Arts et Métiers in Paris and, shortly thereafter, to meet the Polish engineer

Zygmunt Stanislaw Makowski, roof of the pavilion for the board of the UIA Congress in London, designed by Theo Cosby, 1961.

Zygmunt Stanislaw Makowski, roof of the Nodus Center, University of Surrey, Guilford, 1972.

Robert Le Ricolais, pre-tensioned Monkey Saddle, lacquered steel pipe and tension cables, 1958.

Robert Le Ricolais, model of flat roof, 1960.

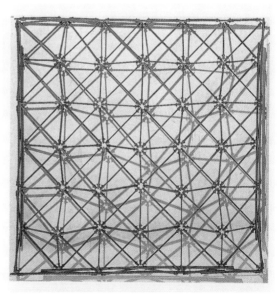

Zygmunt Stanislaw Makowski in London and Robert Le Ricolais in Philadelphia. Piano never tires of emphasizing the importance of these encounters and travels. But since we will have a chance, further on, to remember these encounters and relationships with personalities such as Prouvé, Albini, Louis Kahn, Le Ricolais, and Marco Zanuso, let us shift our focus for a moment to Makowski, who for Piano was, along with Le Ricolais, one of the "true masters," who introduced him to experimentation with spatial structures.

Makowski's books are still listed in the essential bibliographies for engineering students. In 1963, before Piano met him, Makowski published his fundamental *Steel Space Structures*, which would be translated into Italian four years later. Makowski was a remarkable personality who, like so many of the individuals mentioned in this book, directly or indirectly influenced the story of the Centre Pompidou. After 1943 he had been part of the resistance movement against the Germans, who had occupied his native Poland in 1939. In 1946 he studied for a short time at the university in Rome, where he probably would have had the opportunity to attend the lectures of engineer Pier Luigi Nervi, also an outstanding innovator in the field of "structural modelling," then went on to earn his degree in London and began teaching at Imperial College. From 1962 to 1966 Makowski headed the department of civil engineering at what was then the Battersea College of Advanced Technology in London. This is where Piano found him, when assessing the construction solutions and results of the early research he had conducted for the Piano family construction company (led by his father, Carlo, and later his brother Ermanno). In London, Piano thus had the chance to observe the experiments Makowski was conducting on form-resistant structures and prefabricated systems for the construction of domes and grid roofs, aimed at exploiting the reticular effects of shells or membranes. In this study of the behavior of how materials can best perform under stresses, Makowski used computer calculation and, above all, models on different scales. Piano had been grappling with these themes and problems in practice ever since working in Albini's studio and studying at the Polytechnic University in Milan, where he discussed his thesis "Modular Modulation and Coordination" with his tutor Giuseppe Ciribini in 1964, before starting his own architectural practice in Genoa. In these same years Piano worked with Zanuso, who with Eduardo Vittoria was designing the new

Marco Zanuso, study for the roof of the Olivetti factories, c. 1967.

Olivetti factory in Scarmagno (Ivrea), Italy (1962–72), for which Zanuso conceived a reticular structure similar to those studied by Makowski, and where later he used a system of skylights probably designed by Piano, who a few years later contributed to the design of the skylights of another Olivetti factory, built in Harrisburg, Pennsylvania, by Louis Kahn (1967–70).

Reading Makowski's articles on Piano's "plastic structures" and seeing photographs of works that Makowski completed or consulted on, it is evident what drew the thirty-year-old Piano to visit Battersea College in the 1960s. In 1961, for example, for the building designed by Theo Crosby for the Congress of the International Union of Architects in London, Makowski produced a roof grid formed by pyramids whose sides were composed of thin aluminum sheets. Considering the conception and behavior of this roof, it can be seen in relation to the reinforced polyester structure Piano developed in Genoa in 1964–65 with Flavio Marano, which he had decided to subject to load testing in Makowski's own lab, probably along with developing the skylights for the Olivetti factory. Taking other constructions by the Polish engineer into consideration, such as the later Space Structures Research Centre of the University of Surrey (1972), it is easy to see that the elements of his experimentation were not very different from those applied by Zanuso in the first project for the Olivetti factory; and by Piano when he built the woodworking shop for his brother Ermanno in Genoa, or the shells made for the Milan Triennale in 1967, or the Italian Industry Pavilion at the Expo '70 in Osaka (working again with Marano). These constructions tested the validity of different structural types, experiments that also recall Otto's first buildings, which continued to be a source of inspiration for Piano over the years.

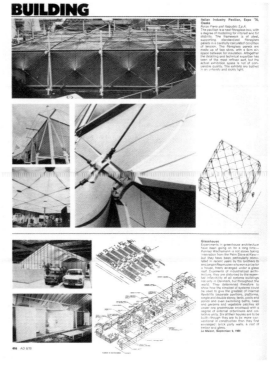

As these works demonstrate, already in the second half of the 1960s, thanks to his work with models Piano was able to design details that made optimal use of the characteristics of materials and resistant frameworks that exploited lightness and increased the strength of structures. As Baltard, Callet, and Joly had done at Paris's Les Halles, and as Makowski (and Zanuso) were doing, from the start of his professional career Piano developed projects focused on experimenting with construction practices that would reduce the weight of structural components and increase the economy of materials. A rational ethos in the use of materials, similar to that which distinguishes economy from chrematistics as Max Weber pointed out, also lies at the base of the conviction that in architecture "elegance," which is an integral aspect of that ethos, "is closely tied to the rigorous necessity of the material," a precocious statement by Piano—echoing Franco Albini, we should note—with which he remained consistent through the years.

So when Rice began to work with Piano, Rogers, and Franchini on the project for Plateau Beaubourg, he did not have to be concerned with finding an answer to the question he was

Architectural Design, August 1970, cover and page 416 presenting Renzo Piano's Italian Industry Pavilion at the Osaka Expo.

raising, as he recalled in *An Engineer Imagines* (the brilliant and instructive posthumously published autobiography written in 1992): how can one combine the creativity of the architect with the innovation of the engineer? "How can we become innovative or creative?" It is plausible to imagine that as Piano approached the Plateau Beaubourg project, it would have been for him a poorly formulated question to ask simply whether it should be one or the other. Between the words "innovative" and "creative" used by Rice, it is likely that Piano perceived the presence of "or" as pleonastic. In practice, what applies to economy and lightness can also apply to creativity and innovation. The two pairs of terms are inseparable in building practice, which begins by "imagining where the forces go" and leads to the set of "qualities that make everything what it is," assigning to calculation, since "creation is never the immediate result of analytical research," a "complementary role" (as it was expressed by Félix Candela, the Spanish architect transplanted to Mexico, inventor and builder of extraordinarily light and thin structures whose name shall reappear soon in these pages).

But when Rice wondered what characterizes the engineer's most "challenging and exciting" work, which requires "the highest skill" in the architect's work, he had not intended to approach a merely theoretical problem, nor to investigate what distinguishes mechanics from statics and composition nor, even more generally, art from science (which only the "practice of architecture" can permit us to resolve, as the eighteenth-century German architect Friedrich Gilly had put forth in one of his enlightening essays). Rice was most interested in returning to the discussion of a question that had also been intensely debated during the nineteenth century. Although Rice probably did not know, in the early 1800s Charles-François Viel, for example, had faced this problem when he addressed the canonical opposition of composition and construction, assigning the latter term an utterly modern meaning in books such as *De l'impuissance des mathématiques pour assurer la solidité des bâtiments* (1805) and *De la solidité des bâtiments* (1806)—books that did not escape the attention of Walter Benjamin more than a century later, between the world wars, when he was unfolding his research on the "archaeology" of modern Paris. Inquiring, more than a century later, about such issues of composition and construction, Rice aimed above all to assess his lived experience, which must be taken into account in order to understand, as *An Engineer Imagines* demonstrates,

his contribution to the construction of Centre Pompidou, working in complete harmony with the Piano and Rogers team in spite of many obstacles. However, to explain the meaning of this assessment and to identify the reasons why the project for Plateau Beaubourg is the outcome of a perfect interpenetration of knowledge and heterodox mentalities—to use the meaning intended by Fuller—we need to take a step back in time.

After having spent a year at Imperial College, Rice entered the firm Ove Arup & Partners in 1956 and after a leave to complete his studies he rejoined the office in 1958. It has yet to be clarified whether Ove Arup directly contacted Jørn Utzon to offer his services as a consultant for the design and construction of the Sydney Opera House or whether jury members of the Australian competition Leslie Martin and Eero Saarinen suggested that the Danish architect turn to the famous London-based Danish engineer. Be that as it may, one of the first jobs assigned to Rice in Ove Arup's studio was work for Utzon's project, whose problematic character had been fully understood by Saarinen, who knew well Fred Severud, in whose office Ted Happold had spent some time. In 1962 Rice went to Sydney to monitor the construction of the Opera House and witnessed the rising tensions, misunderstandings, and clashes that ultimately made the simultaneous presence of the Arup engineers and Utzon on the same worksite impossible. Given this background, one cannot help but wonder how Utzon reacted when a few years later, having turned down for health reasons the invitation to be a member of the Plateau Beaubourg competition jury, he heard that the scheme submitted by Arup with Piano, Rogers, and Franchini was the winner. Putting this mischievous conjecture aside, the fact remains that in 1966 Utzon stepped away from the responsibility for the construction of the Sydney Opera House, making a decision that had significant resonance.

In December 1967 the Madrid-based magazine *Arquitectura* published an essay by Félix Candela, then at the height of his career. The essay, "El escandalo de la Opera de Sydney," contains a painstaking autopsy of what had happened in Sydney from 1956 to 1966. Candela fully agreed with the assessment of Nervi, who believed that Utzon's initial design would have been impossible to build. Examining the reasons behind Utzon's failure, Candela lucidly asserted that the blame should be assigned in equal parts to the architect and the engineers of Ove Arup & Partners. "No one had ever constructed a building of the form and proportions Utzon was proposing, a monumental sculpture on a gigantic scale," Candela wrote, "and no one, including Utzon, had the slightest idea how it could be built." But while it is not unusual for an architect not to know how to implement a design he has created, Candela continued, it is more surprising that Ronald Jenkins, the Arup office's best expert on calculation, had to devote "375,000 hours of work and over 2,000 hours of electronic processing to try to solve a problem that had no solution." Having made these precise considerations, Candela reaches a general conclusion whose tone, so different from the loudness of Fuller's statements for example, also reflects his debt to his intellectual guide since his days at the University of Madrid in the 1930s, the philosopher José Ortega y Gasset: "One of the most extraordinary characteristics of man today, in this era of electronic miracles, of immediate communications, of incredible technological progress and frenetic specialization," Candela wrote, "is his boundless arrogance, as a logical consequence of his boundless ignorance."

Rice had helped write the computer program that was supposed to calculate the behavior of the curved shells and plates that the Arup studio developed for Utzon's Opera House. The future designer of the Centre Pompidou

had followed the path indicated by his expert senior colleague Ronald Jenkins. But Jenkins, Candela observed, was "fascinated by the difficulty of calculation" and while he indulged in "an engaging and pleasant mathematical pastime," he reiterated a worn-out cliché: "The mission of the engineer lies simply in making anything the architect imagines possible, however absurd it might be."

After leaving Sydney and spending several months in the United States, Rice returned to London in 1968. In 1971, in the issue of *Architectural Design* devoted to Otto we have already encountered, Rice wrote a piece that gives us an informed assessment of his firsthand witness of the events that led to Utzon's resignation from the Australian project. Significantly, Rice contrasts the cult of structural simplicity that Otto practiced with Utzon's worship of the "will of form":

> Unlike most architects his [Otto's] approach to form springs from a knowledge of structure rather than a knowledge of sculpture . . . [and] in this sense he is entirely different from Utzon. . . . Utzon seems to know the sculptural form he wants and then sets about, or sets others about, finding how to achieve it. Frei starts with an extensive armory of techniques for producing new forms which have structural simplicity (like most great architect/engineers he is always striving for direct force structures) and a great curiosity to explore more forms. He would never "force" the form to achieve an architectural effect.

Emphasizing how the aesthetic of Otto's constructions comes directly from observation and from parsing the effects of tensions and their static composition, Rice offers an unintentional but clear explanation of the affinity he senses with Piano and Rogers, and how their successful collaboration on the Beaubourg project was facilitated by their shared fundamental design philosophy. The issue of *Architectural Design* devoted to Otto was released in March 1971; a few months later, the project by Piano, Rogers, Franchini, and Ove Arup & Partners was announced as the winner of the competition for Plateau Beaubourg. Like Utzon's design for the Sydney Opera House, Rice explained, "Piano and Rogers' scheme for Beaubourg had a number of features which separated it from all the other entries." But ten years after Utzon's decision to reduce the system of sails of the opera house to a succession of triangles derived from a single sphere, attempting to make an otherwise unsolvable problem approachable (as Rafael Moneo clarified after having worked in Utzon's office), by 1971 Rice and others in the Arup group Structure 3 had learned how to treat a project as unusual as their Plateau Beaubourg submission. That lesson came unintentionally from Jenkins, their senior colleague, who had by example in Sydney indicated the path to avoid. Moreover, the architects Rice collaborated with at the start of 1971 were utterly different from Utzon: like Rice and Happold, Piano and Rogers admired the "structural simplicity" of Otto's works. They were not attracted to sculptural forms and did not see any effective role for opposing "ordonnance et construction," to use terms that had been established even before Viel employed them in his writings in the opening years of the nineteenth century.

What Rice states in the passages quoted above explains one of the many reasons why the construction of the Centre Pompidou was a success—the first of many that Piano, Rogers, and Rice would achieve after its completion. What had happened a few years earlier in Australia helped to set this anchor point in the history of contemporary architecture. This demonstrates that when one works on architectural history it is advisable not to forget the "butterfly effect." Edward Lorenz in the early 1970s introduced this concept in chaos theory, explaining it with the title of one of his well-known lectures: "Does the flap of butterfly's wings in Brazil set off a tornado in Texas?" We can adjust this question for our purposes: "A butterfly's fluttering wings in Australia had significant effects in Paris."

Four years older than Piano, Richard Rogers was born in Florence of Italian parents. His father, like his wife, came from Trieste; he was the cousin of Ernesto N. Rogers, a leading Italian architect active from the 1930s to the 1960s with the office BBPR (Gianluigi Banfi, Ludovico Belgiojoso, Enrico Peressutti, and Ernesto Rogers), and for several years the editor of the influential Italian architecture magazine *Casabella*. Arriving in England at the age of six, following the example of his father's cousin Rogers studied at the Architectural Association School in London and then went to the United States to attend the School of Architecture of Yale University in 1961–62 alongside Norman Foster, and like him was seriously influenced by Fuller. In 1963 after his return from the United States, Rogers founded the Team 4 studio in London

with Foster and his wife, Wendy Cheesman, and Wendy's sister
Georgia. Su Brumwell, Rogers's wife, did not have an architecture degree but still took an active part in the work of the firm.

In 1964 Marcus and Irene Brumwell, Su's parents,
decided to build a house on the English Cornwall coast,
at Feock. Marcus Brumwell headed a multidisciplinary
design and consulting studio, the Design Research Unit
(DRU), and after some initial hesitation he assigned the job
of designing the house to Team 4. The villa, Creek Vean,
was completed in 1966, one year before the studio was dis-
solved. The studio's last characteristically eloquent work
was the Reliance Controls building in Swindon, Wiltshire.
After the Team 4 experience, while they were building a home
for Richard's parents in Wimbledon, in keeping with modes

Renzo Piano and Richard Rogers, 1971.

Team 4, c. 1965. Front row (from left): Sophie Read, Wendy Foster, Richard Rogers, Su Rogers, Norman Foster, Maurice Philips. Standing (from left): Tony Hurt and Frank Peacock.

Team 4, Creek Vean, Feock, Cornwall, 1964–66.

Team 4, Reliance Controls, Swindon, England, 1967.

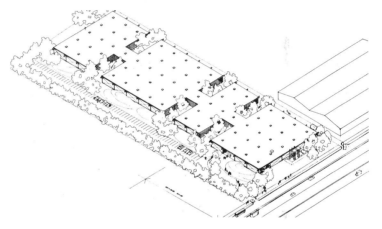

developed in California by architects such as Eero Saarinen, Raphael Soriano, Charles and Ray Eames, and Craig Ellwood after 1945, the Rogers developed, for DRU, a project manifesto commissioned by the chemical company DuPont that takes the name from its construction technique, the Zip-Up House. This was a housing cell, a container using a chassis formed by load-bearing panels composed of aluminum sheets alternating with layers of insulation, held together by zippers—clearly indebted to Fuller and destined to play a role, if not crucial, in the development of the scheme for Centre Pompidou. The first version of the Zip-Up House dates from 1968, and the bright colors proposed for the interiors and the enclosure are similar to the images in the film *Yellow Submarine*, directed by George Dunning and featuring the Beatles and their music, produced

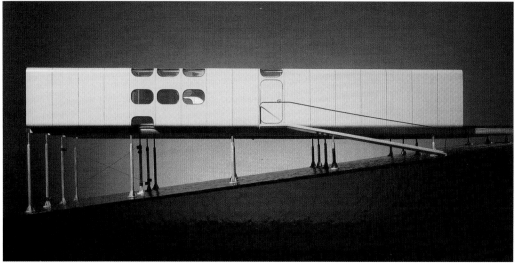

Richard and Su Rogers, Rogers House, London, 1968–69.

Richard Rogers, Zip-Up House, 1968.

that year. Like the air-supported office built in Hertfordshire in 1970 by Norman Foster, the Zip-Up House was representative of the atmosphere of 1960s England and had gained a certain level of renown when Piano returned to London (perhaps to meet again with Makowski) at a time when he did not yet know Rogers: after all, as proven by the Creek Vean house and, more explicitly, the Reliance Controls building, even though their paths had not yet overlapped they were tending to follow the same compass. Piano and Rogers did not meet until later, when a doctor who was treating Richard for a childhood disease transmitted from one of his children chanced to put them into contact. In spite of the extemporaneous character of this first encounter, it is easy to see how an understanding developed between Piano and Rogers that soon moved toward their collaboration in the Piano & Rogers studio, not disbanded until 1976, when Piano formed a partnership with Rice.

After moving to London, Piano began teaching at the Architectural Association and the Polytechnic of Central London. He came to the attention of Monica Pidgeon, the influential editor of *Architectural Design* from 1946 to 1975, and the magazine covered his work in the March 1970 issue. In the meantime, Piano began to frequent London architecture circles, with which Rogers already had more familiarity. Like all such environments, London included certain personalities who set the tone more than others. Outstanding examples included Alison and Peter Smithson, Warren Chalk, Peter Cook, Dennis Crompton, David Greene, Ron Herron, and Mike Webb, involved in Archigram; architects such as James Stirling; and historians John Summerson, director of Sir John Soane's Museum; and Reyner Banham, working for *Architectural Review*. Like Cedric Price, they were all more or less connected with the Architectural Association.

Price was a particularly intelligent and brilliant man, and notably worldly and snobbish. For instance, although they had opposing political ideas, he was fast friends with the preeminent London developer Alastair McAlpine, who would become treasurer of the Conservative Party under Prime Minister Margaret Thatcher in 1979. And, though without particular enthusiasm for the theater, Price was a friend of Joan Littlewood, the tutelary deity of action and propaganda theater, who in turn was scarcely interested in architecture. The Soviet propaganda trains of the 1920s and the Berliner Ensemble created by Bertolt Brecht in East Berlin were her points of reference. "An extraordinary mixture of the ham and social conscience," according to Banham, Littlewood had begun her career in the early 1930s in the Workers Theatre Movement; after 1945 she had founded the Theatre Workshop and was connected with the Communist Party.

As Stanley Mathews wrote in *From Agit-Prop to Free Space: The Architecture of Cedric Price* (2007), in 1962 Littlewood met Price, twenty years her junior. The result of their meeting was the project of the "first giant mobile space in the world," whose conception and aims made it the most telling expression of the iconoclastic and provocative attitude shared at the time by a segment of English architectural culture. The project in question was called the Fun Palace, and in the early 1960s it played out, deposited on paper in a range of versions, in the vain hope of finding a suitable place to land and money for construction. The Fun Palace confirms that Rem Koolhaas was effectively curt when in the book *Re: CP* (2003), edited by Hans Ulrich Obrist, he wrote, "Price wanted to deflate architecture to the point where it became indistinguishable from the ordinary. . . . Price cut a huge swath through the thicket of architectural illusions that architecture still maintained in the fifties and sixties. Ironically his scorched earth became the fertile fields for a still on-going Anglo-Saxon triumph: Archigram, Rogers, Foster, Alsop." Fun Palace consisted of a spatial structure that offered a range of services whose purpose was to stimulate intelligent and formative use of leisure time. From this design and study derives its historical meaning: as the point from which Price and Littlewood started their work devoted to time free from work. As a leisure facility, the Fun Palace signaled the numerous changes of social attitudes and of economic juncture at the beginning of the 1960s that proved Great Britain had finally recovered from the restrictions, shortages, and scarcities that had accompanied World War II and its aftermath.

Littlewood and Price's idea of the Fun Palace was to create a "large shipyard in which enclosures such as theatres, cinemas, restaurants, workshops, rally areas, can be assembled, moved, rearranged, and scrapped continuously." As Price explained, "its mechanically operated environmental controls are such that it can be sited in a hard, dirty, industrial area unsuited to more conventional types of amenity buildings." In a construction that, in Banham's words, "as an enclosure provides only a roof over one's head," technology, movement,

Cedric Price, Fun Palace, 1960–65; interior perspective; the model (Canadian Centre for Architecture).

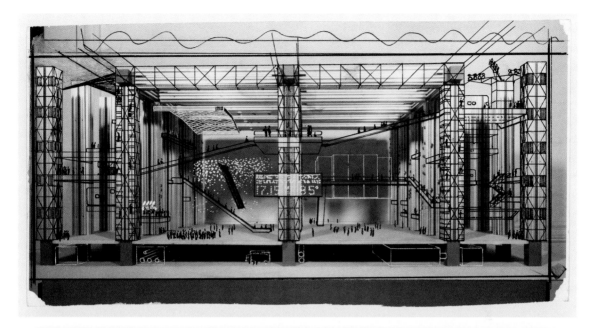

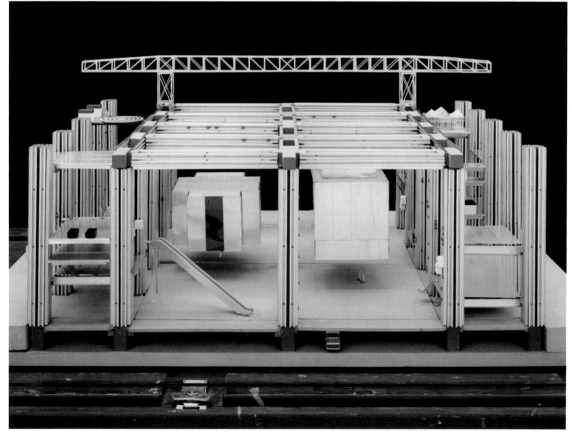

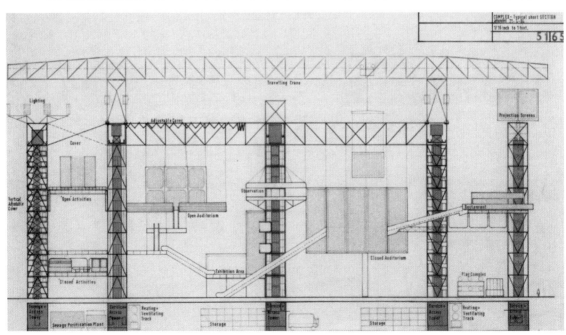

Lighting

Travelling Crane

Projection Screens

Adjustable Cover

Cover

Vertical Adjustable Cover

Open Activities

Observation

Open Auditorium

Restaurant

Closed Auditorium

Exhibition Area

Play Complex

Closed Activities

Sewage Access Tower

Service Access Tower

Heating + Ventilating Track

Service Access Tower

Service Access Tower

Heating + Ventilating Track

Service Access Tower

Sewage Purification Plant

Storage

Storage

fungibility, and communications gear relegated architecture, in the traditional sense of the term—namely what is commonly intended as a building—to an ancillary role. A framework of reticular beams was intentionally organized in an essential way thanks to the contribution of a leading English engineer, Frank Newby, who later contributed (it is worth remembering) to the construction of the Aviary in Regent's Park Zoo in London, which Price designed with Lord Snowdon, and of the Engineering Building of the Leicester University, designed by James Stirling and James Gowan. The structure Price conceived with Newby would have permitted "a flow of space and time, in which passive and active pleasure is provoked," where "the varied and ever-changing activities will determine the form of the site." This said, following Mathews's retracing of the history of this project, it comes as no surprise to learn that since Price's university days in the 1950s, first at Cambridge and then in London at the Architectural Association, he had taken Buckminster Fuller as one of his models. Adopting Fuller's panache, he thought of himself as an "anti-architect" and of the Fun Palace as an "anti-building," a place "where the latest discoveries of engineering and science can provide an environment for pleasure and discovery."

Price and Littlewood saw the terms "learning" and "leisure" as almost synonyms and had imagined the Fun Palace, not by chance conceived to be built outside of the representative and historical town, as an explicit critique of the existing education system ("designed merely to perpetuate the status quo"), a polemical alternative to cultural institutions like museums, which the pair believed were "forms in which human energy can no longer be contained." Designing Beaubourg, Piano and Rogers also used the words "fun," "leisure," and "learning" with meanings similar to those assigned to them by Price and Littlewood, and spoke of the center as a "university of the streets." But rather than the configuration of the Fun Palace, which Banham called "a mechanized temple for Homo Ludens," it was the conceptual framework and ideological implications of their proposals that made Littlewood and Price the "background of Pompidou," as Rogers has frankly acknowledged. But if there is no reason to mistrust Rogers's statement, it is also appropriate to notice the differences between the architectural approaches of Price, from one side, and of Piano and Rogers, from the other. This becomes clear if we consider, for instance, the project for a standard hospital

45   Butterfly Effects

module prepared by Piano & Rogers in 1970–71 for the Association of Rural Aids in Medicine (ARAM) on a commission by the World Bank. Often cited as proof of the influence of the designer of the Fun Palace, this project discloses a deep difference, and in any case cannot be traced back to Price's intentions and expressive modes. The Piano & Rogers hospital module project in fact was an exercise in standardization associated with the study of an integrated, constraining construction method, and it has little in common with the anti-architecture of Price or with the "clip-on or plug-in architecture" in vogue in those days in Europe and elsewhere. Banham—with these curious terms he had coined in the essay "A Clip-on Architecture" (*Architectural Design*, November 1965), and who, however, considered the ARAM module "a plausible progenitor of Centre Pompidou"—defined the rather widespread fashion of the time of clipping on or plugging in appendages of different types to make very uniform structures function in different ways. This approach was in keeping with a design strategy that does not trace back to the technique of assembly, which as we have seen gives to Centre Pompidou its essential form.

The background of the project for Plateau Beaubourg is also usually associated with something that began in 1961 with the circulation of the pamphlet *Archigram* in the architectural and more sophisticated intellectual circles in London. Archigram was a neo-technological avant-garde group whose attitude was deeply influenced by Fuller's ideas and Otto's experiences. Linked to the Architectural Association, Archigram was supported by the magazine *Architectural Design*, where Theo Crosby, who worked with Makowski, had been involved under Monica Pidgeon's editorship. Archigram's pamphlets and production quickly evolved "from a student fanzine into something halfway between a spatial architecture comic book and a protest journal," as Banham summarized the evolution of the group. Yet as Alain Guiheux has written in the Centre Pompidou exhibition catalogue *Archigram* (1994), the architects who had given life to this experience, not unlike Price, integrated "in their projects the universe of the society of consumption, its seductive, colorful and ephemeral goods, supermarkets and their pop aesthetic, rock 'n' roll and the Beatles, the garish colors of advertising, the early developments of data processing and new communications media, the space shots and the first steps on the

Piano & Rogers, hospital module designed for the Association of Rural Aids in Medicine (ARAM), 1970–71.

Moon." For these reasons too, Rogers thought that, unlike the Fun Palace, "Archigram seemed disturbingly apolitical."

Beyond the different political undertones of the Price and Archigram projects mentioned by Rogers, there are other reasons why the Fun Palace rests more securely in the background of Beaubourg than the projects conceived by Archigram. While Fun Palace objectively sets a precedent for Centre Pompidou's conception, this is not due to the fact that both projects envisioned non-buildings, as some have claimed. If Price imagined Fun Palace as a place in continuous transformation, determined by a spatial platform destined to play out its function in the very moment in which the construction was completed, Centre Pompidou represents quite the opposite. The Piano and Rogers building has a permanent, stable character whose purpose is to display the "making" of its "forms that make an assault on space . . . constructed not from aesthetics, but from material," as El Lissitzky had stated fifty years earlier when speaking of the Russian Constructivists (an "object of desire" in Europe and in London during the 1960s), using words the designers of Centre Pompidou could easily have made their own. While no enclosure was envisioned for Fun Palace, the elevations of Centre Pompidou are the result of a very careful exercise of composition, as Jean Prouvé has emphasized, aimed at harmonizing the various tensions that cross it, generated by the statics of the structures and the visibility of the volume of technical apparatus, where in a rather constructivist way "color is used as a barometer of the material," to quote El Lissitzky again. The building, moreover, has the look of a fixed set installed around a diffused stage, where there is a continually renewed performance of the mutably transient, of the ordinary that alights there, of the ephemeral that passes through. In this way, the Centre Pompidou is like a gigantic arcade in a tradition of Parisian arcades. It is similar to the market passages covered in iron and glass roofs built in Paris since the beginning of the nineteenth century, several of which were destroyed with Haussmann's redesign of Paris. They were the haunts of Parisian *flâneurs*, the curious and fashionable strollers immortalized by Baudelaire and again through Benjamin, who wrote, "As long as gas and even oil lamps were burning in them, [the arcades] were fairytale palaces." No longer in the bowels of the city, Plateau Beaubourg is invaded by the lights and colors of advertising, opened up to embrace a vast

Ron Herron, model for Instant City, 1970.

plaza. But "the passing, the being-no-longer, works passionately in things, and the monuments of a being-no-longer are the passages, and nothing of them lasts except the name" in which is distilled "the present as the inner essence of what has been." This observation by Benjamin is so sparkling it can be adopted to illuminate the meaning of Centre Pompidou today.

Archigram's captivating projects were not only ideologically ambiguous, they were also manifestations of a cult of representation taken to the point of assigning the task of metaphorically "dismissing technology," ironic masks of papier mâché soaked in instant impressions. Archigram, Banham wrote in 1965, is in fact not capable of explaining how the projects it presents will function, but "definitely knows how to describe their appearance." This production of rhetorically alternative projects that pleasantly filled the pages of English avant-garde magazines in the 1960s would be "perfectly possible tomorrow, if only the universe (and especially the Law of Gravity) were differently organized," Banham quipped in his 1966 article "Zoom Wave Hits Architecture." Such projects are worlds apart from the Centre Pompidou. In the building by Piano, Rogers, Franchini, and Rice, structural components and constructive details play decisive roles; the tectonic arrangement is displayed and becomes the protagonist of the architecture's narrative, which takes form from the continuous contest between weight and the law of gravity. In Ron Herron's Instant City project, an outstanding example of Archigram production, on the other hand, the roofs are lovingly raised from the ground by the thrust of multicolored hot-air balloons, representations of forces that can only be thought capable of defying Newton's Second Law if they are construed as humor.

Peter Cook, Plug-In University Node, 1965.

Archigram 4, cover, 1964.

Chapter Three
The Competition: The President, the Jury, and the Jesters

Reyner Banham published the article "Zoom Wave Hits Architecture" in the March 3, 1966, issue of *New Society*; the same year, *Time* announced that "in a decade dominated by youth, London has burst into bloom. It swings: it is the scene." The liveliness of this scene had not faded when at the end of 1970 or the start of 1971 Ted Happold convinced his colleagues at Ove Arup & Partners that participation in the competition for Plateau Beaubourg was an opportunity not to be missed.

With that settled, however, Happold had to make another decision, one that was more complicated. The competition was only for architects, and in the beginning of 1971 Ove Arup & Partners, which was an engineering office, had to decide which architects they would join forces with to develop their entry. Considering his options, in the awareness of how important it could be for the firm's internal group Structure 3 to take part in a prestigious competition like the one organized by the Délégation pour la Réalisation du Centre du Plateau Beaubourg, the public body created for the construction of the center, Happold recalled an episode from just one year earlier. As Nathan Silver relates in *The Making of Beaubourg* (1994), in 1969 Rogers, as he himself explained on several occasions, had contacted Frei Otto, asking him to collaborate on a project for the Chelsea Football Club. Otto was not able to take part and had suggested that the young English architect get in touch with Structure 3. Having become acquainted in this way, Happold turned to Rogers and proposed entering the Paris competition together, combining the resources of the studio recently formed with Piano with the greater financial and technical solidity of Ove Arup & Partners. Su Rogers and Piano, also seeing an advantage in the economic contribution Ove Arup & Partners was willing to provide, quickly convinced Richard to abandon the British skepticism with which he greeted the idea of such a French adventure. Thus in the first months of 1971 work began on the project; the submission deadline was June 15. The initial project team was small. Besides Piano, Su

Portrait collage of the members of the London and Genoa studios during the development of the project for Plateau Beaubourg, 1972.

and Richard Rogers, Franchini, Peter Rice, Happold, Lennart Grut, John Young, and Marco Goldschmied were in the group, joined on a more or less regular basis by Peter Flack and Jan Kaplicky. We can consider them to be the authors of the scheme that reached Paris in an entry that would become inventory number 493, of the 681 projects accepted by the jury.

The competition guidelines can easily be summed up from what was published in the February 1977 issue of *L'Architecture d'aujourd'hui* and in Silver's book. The building had to supply 692,120 square feet (64,300 square meters) of above-ground area, 75,347 square feet (7,000 square meters) of free spaces, and 269,000 square feet (25,000 square meters) of underground parking. Furthermore, 53,820 square feet (5,000 square meters) were set aside for the Institut de Recherche et Coordination Acoustique/Musique (IRCAM). In 1970 President Georges Pompidou indeed decided to entrust the direction of IRCAM to the conductor and composer Pierre Boulez, deeming it worthwhile, as Pompidou's wife Claude urged, to bring him back to Paris from his self-imposed "exile" following disagreements with former Minister of Culture André Malraux several years earlier. In addition to library and museum areas, the largest zones were earmarked for temporary exhibitions, documentation centers, and industrial creation. Piano, Rogers, and Franchini planned to distribute these freely inside a five-story construction, 558 feet long and 164 feet wide (170 by 50 meters), aligned with a large open space. Work began in March 1972, and at the conclusion of construction, the area of the facility would reach a total of 1,111,965 square feet (103,305 square meters), and the cost of the building—not estimated in the guidelines—would reach 727.3 million francs, again according to reports in *L'Architecture d'aujourd'hui*. Especially in the years from 1974 to 1977, such an investment would absorb a major portion of the funds available to the French public administration, including those set aside for cultural activities in general. After 1974 this fact would lead President Valéry Giscard d'Estaing—whom we cannot consider a whole-hearted supporter of the construction of the center commemorating his predecessor—to repeatedly attempt, with a certain amount of success, to reduce the funding commitments, reaching the point of seriously threatening the prospects of completing the work.

According to Piano and Rogers, behind their project lay the intention to challenge the goals of the guidelines of the competition, seen as too "formal and monumental." Instead of "a 'container' for art, we propose the construction of a building for information, fun and culture, a sort of machine, an 'informative tool,'" they later wrote in *L'Architecture d'aujourd'hui*. This demonstrates that the "philosophy" they adopted and to some extent the function they imagined for Beaubourg was not substantially different from the one Cedric Price and Joan Littlewood saw for the Fun Palace a few years earlier. The implicit goal of their project, conceived "in the spirit of '68," as Piano said, was to make an ideology plausible, to which Price had attempted to grant a form, and to make it possible to construct a provocation, that which Archigram had managed to represent graphically.

But as proof of the fact that the orientation indicated by President Charles de Gaulle in 1968 to the ministers of his government—"reform yes, masquerade no"—had not gone unheeded, in the summer of 1971 Piano and Rogers's provocative intent still caused little controversy. Pompidou and those in his circle favored a celebration of culture and the implementation of modern cultural policy, seeing it as a valid alternative to the anarchy that in their view had reigned in Paris in May 1968, threatening to become an epidemic. This is why the center they imagined, as Louis Pinto has written in *Décostruire Beaubourg* (1991), was "a transgression of hierarchies that is now considered legitimate," aimed at fostering "creativity" through "lively interdisciplinary action" practiced by means of "participation, dialogue, and free expression." These words so often heard in the debates that had taken place in May 1968 in the universities, on the stage of the Théâtre de l'Odéon and elsewhere, had now been absorbed by the highest institutions of the state, which set out to transfer them into the "philosophy of the Centre" for which the architects were asked to provide an "architectural translation." Given these premises, the client imagined the building as "a flexible structure and a dynamic tool of communication, capable of attracting the largest possible audience, overcoming the limitations traditionally imposed on culture by institutions." Similar indications were expressed in different but not contradictory ways by the various protagonists of the story we are reconstructing. The amusing slogan with which Pontus Hultén, appointed by supervisor of the project Robert Bordaz as director of the center's Department of Arts while the building was still under construction, expressively and precisely summed up the task at hand: "We need to take the uniforms off the guards and the culture"—a slogan that clearly echoes those coined in the Spring of 1968.

In the meantime, in July 1971 eight of the nine members of the jury charged with choosing the winner of the competition expressed approval of the project by Piano, Rogers, Franchini, and the Structure 3 group of Arup & Partners, whose roots probed into the "outlaw areas" of which Buckminster Fuller spoke and which Paris, still reeling from the effects of May 1968, found fertile ground. And this was not due to the fact that "jesters are always permitted to make fun of the powerful," as Piano asserted with a certain amount of smug ingenuousness, but instead—were it not equally ingenuous to think so—just the opposite. For in this case, perhaps the power, through the construction of Centre Pompidou, was making fun of the jesters. The truth was actually simpler: "The project by Piano, Rogers, and Ove Arup," Jean Prouvé would say in 1977, "responded masterfully to the program, and the job of the jury was to respect that program."

The jury completed its deliberations in ten days in July 1971; it was formed by people well versed in the tasks the building would fulfill, even more so if we consider the fact that the most important functions to be housed in the center were exhibition spaces and a library. The chairman of the jury was Prouvé; no one deserved such a role more than he, and no one would have been capable of so impeccably judging a project like the one submitted by Piano, Rogers, Franchini, and Structure 3. Furthermore, Prouvé had participated in the construction of the Maison du Peuple in Clichy (1938), experimenting with solutions designed to produce a "mechanization of space" that had not escaped the attention of Piano or Rogers. The vice chairman of the jury was Gaëtan Picon. After being part of the anti-German French Resistance—as were many of the protagonists involved in this story—during the war, he was editor of *Mercure de France*; but more importantly, as he was in charge of the division of Arts and Letters of the Ministry of Culture, Picon was one of the policymakers pursued by Malraux who aimed to give every major French city its own Maison de la Culture. Émile Aillaud taught at the École Nationale Supérieure des Beaux-Arts; a designer of various housing developments, he had Pompidou's esteem and was involved in the programs for the transformation of La Defénse, west of Paris, in what was to be one of the largest business districts in Europe, and of

The competition jury for Plateau Beaubourg, 1971. Seated (from left): Oscar Niemeyer, Frank Francis, Jean Prouvé, Émile Aillaud, Philip Johnson, Willem Sandberg (back turned).

Philip Johnson while serving on the competition jury for Plateau Beaubourg, 1971, in front of a presentation board featuring the design by Renzo Piano, Richard Rogers, Gianfranco Franchini, and Ove Arup & Partners.

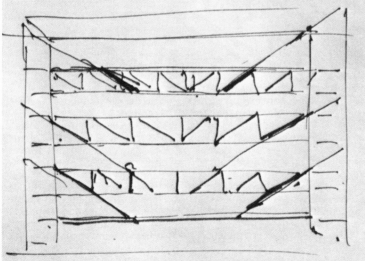

Les Halles; he can be seen as one of the suspects for the lone vote against the project by Piano, Rogers, Franchini, and Ove Arup & Partners. Frank Francis was a noted librarian, associated with various innovative transformations at the British Museum, where he had been director from 1959 to 1968. Philip Johnson played a leading role on the international architecture scene; he was well known for his initiatives at the Museum of Modern Art in New York from the start of the 1930s, his renowned Glass House in Connecticut (1949), his relationship with the master of modern architecture Ludwig Mies van der Rohe, and his successful professional practice in New York. Michel Laclotte was the successor to Germain Bazin heading the department of paintings at the Louvre; as general director, he had then reorganized the museum in keeping with the desires of Malraux; shortly thereafter he would be involved in the transformation of the Gare d'Orsay into a museum. Herman Liebaers was a linguist and an esteemed librarian; director of the Bibliothèque Royale of Brussels in 1954, he had taken Jørn Utzon's place on the jury after the latter's withdrawal; Liebaers is our second suspect as the culprit for the lack of unanimity in the jury's decision. Oscar Niemeyer was the designer of Brasilia; after the coup that brought the military to power in Brazil in 1964, without neglecting his work in Brazil he had opened a studio in Paris; in 1971 he was involved in the construction of the headquarters of the French Communist Party in Paris, and he was working on the design for Le Havre's Maison de la Culture. Willem Sandberg, who during World War II had been engaged in protecting Jews in occupied Netherlands, belonged to the neo-Zoroastrian sect Mazdaznan; he was a good graphic artist and when asked to be part of the jury of the Plateau Beaubourg competition it had been some time since he had left the position of director of the Stedelijk Museum in Amsterdam, which he had profoundly transformed. The auxiliary member of the jury was Henri-Pierre Maillard, a student of the architect André Lurçat and teacher at the École Nationale Supérieure des Beaux-Arts. Sébastien Loste, who prepared the competition announcement, was the secretary.

The members of the jury felt that the new cultural center should respond to an imperative and have characteristics that were considered inviolable: the building, they stated, should not be a "monument." Inevitably they wound up appreciating the project by Piano, Rogers, Franchini, and Ove Arup &

Partners, which although unusual seemed to point to a construction that was "linear, flexible, functional, multipurpose," and above all—and this is the key word used by the jurors to defend their choice—"simple." Actually none of these terms, if used to describe the qualities or characteristics of a work of architecture, never mind a project, has a precise or unequivocal meaning. Just as it is truly complicated to determine on the basis of what values or principles a construction can be considered a monument, it is equally hard to define the criteria with which to start to assign shared meanings to expressions like simplicity, linearity, flexibility, and functionality. But it is the indeterminate, precarious, and imprecise nature of these words that makes it impossible to use them as objective and shared parameters of judgment, although they are part of the vocabulary of the competition's guidelines. This explains in part why the jury chose the Piano, Rogers, Franchini, and Arup project, reaching an intrinsically paradoxical verdict. In fact, as we will now see, if the construction of the Centre Pompidou had not been identified by the supposed simplicity the jury felt was the crucial trait of the winning proposal, we might also wonder to what extent the current building responds to the jury's most insistent prescriptive: that it must not be a new monument in Paris. Agreeing that it wasn't one, paradoxically the jurors chose the project they found most reassuring, and one that was certainly not designed with this goal.

The design by Piano and Rogers called for a building that perhaps would have brought an atmosphere similar to that of New York's Times Square to the center of Paris—free of the stability, fixity, and eloquence that, as the cult of clichés would have it, represent the distinctive traits of what is usually considered a monument. But monuments, as Alois Riegl had explained, are not easy to catalogue, and it is not true that "Architecture is always a set of actual monuments" as stated by Henry-Russell Hitchcock and Philip Johnson in their influential book *The International Style* (1932), published along with the first architecture exhibition at the Museum of Modern Art, New York, "Modern Architecture: International Exhibition." Riegl, writing in the late nineteenth century, not only contributed the modern definition of the tasks of the history of art and its methods of investigation with his theory of the *Denkmalkultus* (cult of the monument), he made an essential contribution to the definition of the role and nature of modern institutions devoted to the preservation of historical heritage and artistic patrimony. At the center of Riegl's theory of values (the process that allows definition of the specific values to be assigned to the material byproducts of a historical development, and then permits establishment of what of the past must be preserved and how), there is the investigation of the same idea of monument, of its nature and meaning. In spite of the fact that his most important contributions about the cult of monuments had been conceived between the nineteenth and twentieth centuries, Riegl's approach to defining the monument is still relevant and can illuminate in what sense the Centre Pompidou is a monument. Monuments, Riegl explained, are always subject to the "deviations that make history" (similar to the events we have attempted thus far to untangle of which Centre Pompidou is the result). These deviations, along with "becoming and passage," which are intrinsic features of the movement of history, mean that monuments can be intentional and commemorative, Riegl explained, created for the purpose of keeping alive "human actions or destinies in the awareness of future generations," or they can be "historical-artistic," free of "a commemorative value, but bearers of a documentary value of the present." Or, finally, Riegl continued, monuments can be "involuntary," expressions of "values of use and novelty" assigned to them by the course of events, and thanks to the relationship established with them by those who observe or "use" them. In any case, "the sense and meaning of monuments are not granted to works in keeping with their original purpose; instead we, the modern subjects, attribute those meanings to the works," assigning them, Riegl concludes, echoing the contents of his extraordinary book *Das holländische Gruppenporträt* (1902), a "value that as memory adheres to the idea of time." The time and the value of novelty—which in our example millions of visitors since 1977 have acknowledged—have very rapidly transformed the Centre Pompidou into precisely what its designers did *not* want it to be: a monument, albeit an involuntary monument.

Rice defined the Centre Pompidou as a "popular palace of culture." In spite of the fact, pointed out by Marc Fumaroli, that Pompidou's mission to build the Centre du Plateau Beaubourg in many ways put an end "to the more severe, more republican 'Malraux mission'" that after 1968 was being "defined in whispers as 'Quixotic,'" the words used by Rice to explain its nature demonstrate that the center was nonetheless also the product of a well-rooted tradition that the Ministry of Culture under de Gaulle had embraced and developed. In fact, it is thanks to the work of Malraux—appointed minister in 1959 with a decree that assigned him the task of "guaranteeing access to our cultural heritage for the widest possible audience and favoring the creation of artworks and the ingenuity that enrich that heritage," as Fumaroli asserted—that culture could become "the name of the state religion in France," and the creed of the "modernity of state" that accompanied it sagaciously cultivated, as was also proven by the philosophy the Centro Pompidou was called upon to interpret. As Fumaroli recalled in *L'État culturel* (1991), an incisive and original book that displays his stimulating intelligence, it was Malraux who launched the plan calling for the construction of a series of cultural centers, "maisons de la culture," across the entire country. Seeing this as a phase of a process destined to make the French society "organic," Picon, whom we met as one of the judges of the Plateau Beaubourg competition, made a decisive contribution to the development and implementation of this program based on an established conviction: "No culture is created by the people, but all culture is created for the people." So the *maisons de la culture* were conceived as places to "offer the means of perfect expression in the field of theater, music, cinema, the plastic arts, literary, scientific, and human knowledge," equipped with all the best tools to "bear constant witness to the activities in the different sectors, to encourage specific cultural promotion in every place, to stimulate cooperation and exchange." "Pyramids and nurseries at the same time," according to an official document issued by the ministry assigned to Malraux in 1962, the *maison de la culture* would "go down in history to show how our country was the first to attempt collective cultural promotion."

When Georges Pompidou "takes things in hand" he does so by renewing the political implications of this project. But his path had begun to take shape even before Malraux and Picon set out on it with such resolve. To trace back briefly this path can help us better understand how deeply the decision to build Beaubourg Pompidou took in 1969 grounded its roots in the recent history of France, placing it in a more inclusive perspective, wider than that offered by the events of May 1968.

Among the many photographs that show Malraux with Le Corbusier—older than those that preserve the memory of Malraux uttering "farewell my old master, my old friend" before the architect's coffin on September 1, 1965, in the Cour

Oscar Niemeyer, Maison de la Culture, Le Havre, 1971–82.

Le Corbusier, Maison de la Culture et de la Jeunesse, Firminy, France, begun 1965.

Carrée of the Louvre—one picture from the start of the 1960s, shot in the architect's studio on rue des Sèvres in Paris, shows the minister and the author of the Chapelle Notre Dame du Haut in Ronchamp studying some drawings. At the time, Le Corbusier was working on the project his collaborators André Wogenscky and Pierre Guariche would posthumously complete in the summer of 1969. It was the Maison de la Culture et de la Jeunesse that the mayor of Firminy, Eugène Claudius-Petit—a man of the Resistance and the former minister of reconstruction with whom Bordaz had worked after the war, as we have seen—had commissioned some time earlier from Le Corbusier. The conjunction of the terms "culture" and "jeunesse" (youth) for Le Corbusier's building is particularly significant and offers a clear indication that the policy Malraux implemented had roots in prewar France, in the years of the Popular Front when between 1936 and 1938 the socialist and communist parties governed the country, and then under the Vichy government. From 1940 to 1942, when Marshal Philippe Pétain was at the helm of the collaborationist government of German-occupied France, the association Jeune France was active, guided by Emmanuel Mounier, the theorist of "communitarian personalism." Since the war years, Mounier too had been thinking about a network of cultural centers as the generator of a national upheaval that could revitalize France after the war. Jeune France, ambiguously oriented toward exalting youth, was a decisive step, in spite of its short life, toward the cultural policy adopted by the Fifth Republic created by de Gaulle in 1958. As Fumaroli has written, it aimed to bring France a new "lay religion, the most foreign to the urgings of Rousseau," devoted to the worship of culture, officially administered by the state; and this would indeed happen with the founding of Malraux's ministry.

When Centre Pompidou was inaugurated by President d'Estaing on January 31, 1977, this trajectory of events we have summarized so far reached its apex. Furthermore, what was happening in France, a country where, as Fumaroli has stated, "people stand at attention at the mere mention of the word *modern*," was just one episode in a process that was destined to have a global impact. Among the many museums and culture palaces built later in tribute to the creed that had spread over the last half century in France, Centre Pompidou offers the best illustration of a deeper, more vast change, in which Malraux's work was but one of the symptoms, though a very evident one, developed after 1968. In 1983 Jean Clair, previously the director of the Musée Picasso in Paris and curator of several important exhibitions organized at Centre Pompidou, described this global change effectively in "Considérations sur l'état des beaux-arts": "At the dawn of the second millennium the monk Glaber marveled at the 'white mantle of churches' that spread across Europe, . . . [and] at the end of the same millennium one might wonder at the gray mantle of museums covering the Western world. In the eleventh century the cult of relics had accelerated the construction of abbeys and established new lines of communication. Today the cult of artworks drives the construction of new temples and regulates the large cultural migrations of tourism."

An engine of the spread and practice of this cult, the Centre Pompidou is now but a pale version of what Mounier and Malraux intended the *maisons de la culture* to be. While the fact that the Centre Pompidou contained a prestigious contemporary art museum made it different, its architectural configuration made it unique—a demonstration that "the entrance of an object into the sphere of the fetish is always the sign of a transgression of the rule that assigns an appropriate use to each thing," as Giorgio Agamben wrote in *Stanzas* (1977).

But having said this, these quick notes do not adequately explain the meanings embodied in the building by Piano, Rogers, Franchini, and Rice. We will now have to approach other issues in order to understand the reasons why Beaubourg is a manifestation of "singularity" and hence "a monster," one of those objects that, as philosopher and cultural theorist Jean Baudrillard explained, "escape from their programming, from the project that has been prepared for them."

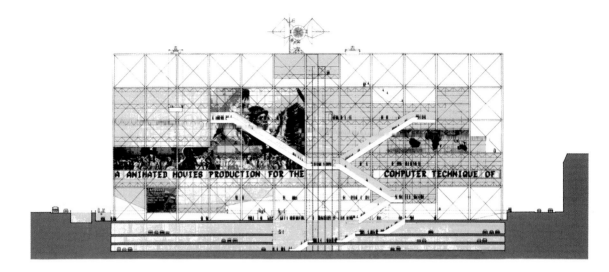

Chapter Four
A Legitimate Transgression

On July 15, 1971, the project by Piano, Rogers, Franchini, and Ove Arup & Partners was announced as the winner of the competition. The guidelines slated completion of the building by the end of 1975. Astonished and unprepared, as Nathan Silver has recounted with endearing openness, the designers soon found themselves in a meeting with the French president at the Elysée. From this moment, not only for them, the hands of the clock started to spin rapidly forward.

The project that had so impressed Jean Prouvé and Philip Johnson rapidly changed its appearance. A studio was set up in Paris. Over time it was to grow, employing about thirty young people of eleven different nationalities. Their design for the Centre Pompidou implied preparation of some 25,000 drawings required to build it, as Silver has noted. After having met the president, the first agreement reached with Robert Bordaz, representative for the client, required that in six months Piano, Rogers, Franchini, Happold, and Rice had to be ready with an *avant-projet sommaire*, a preliminary synopsis and plan of the practical steps. The signing of the contract to seal this agreement was the first step on a difficult path that would also lead to rewriting the old ways of regulating the architectural profession in France.

According to Piano and Rogers, the *avant-projet sommaire* called for "an audiovisual piece" rather than "an architecture." The location of the building on the site was the same as indicated in the competition scheme: the construction, as today, was placed against rue du Renard to the east and opened onto a vast plaza to the west. In the first design, the volume of the building was raised off the ground, and the plaza extended under the building, making it perfectly permeable. The continuous movement of people would accompany the always-changing information that along with graphic effects would mark the main facade, a gigantic screen where all sorts of images could flow. The facade recalled similar experiments that had been conducted since the 1920s and 1930s, but on a larger scale, and reactivated in the 1960s. The architects and engineers proposed an apparatus that was

Renzo Piano, Richard Rogers, Gianfranco Franchini, Ove Arup & Partners, competition design for Plateau Beaubourg, 1971.

Renzo Piano, Richard Rogers, Gianfranco
Franchini, Ove Arup & Partners, models
built after winning the competition for
Plateau Beaubourg.

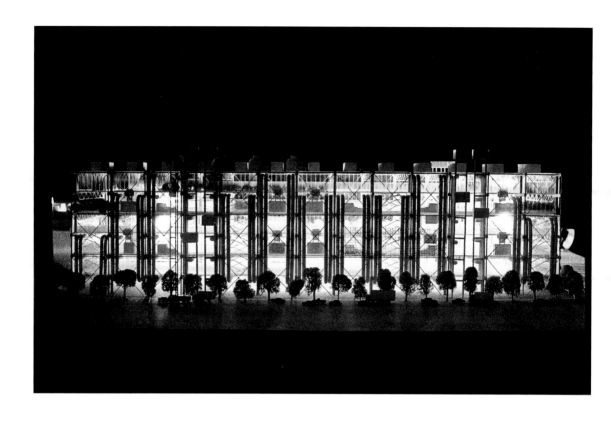

Renzo Piano, Richard Rogers, Gianfranco
Franchini, Ove Arup & Partners, model
built after winning the competition for
Plateau Beaubourg.

Vladimir Tatlin, exhibition poster featuring the model of the Monument to the Third International, 1920.

Aleksandr Rodchenko, Design for a Kiosk, 1919.

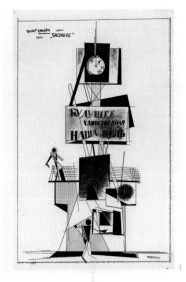

an extreme attempt to make architecture speak. Were we to seek its origins, without going too far afield, we would think of the celebrated French architects of the eighteenth century—Étienne-Louis Boullée rather than Claude-Nicolas Ledoux, even though the latter's work was identified by Anthony Vidler in the book he devoted to the French architect as "speaking architecture." But in order to avoid going back so far, the most plausible ancestors of the scheme presented in 1971 are more recent and numerous. They include, for example, Vladimir Tatlin, Aleksandr Rodchenko, and Soviet architects and designers who after 1917 set themselves the task of making propaganda "at the service of the Revolution"; Herbert Bayer and his compositions incorporating advertising; Erich Mendelsohn and his architectures of light; Oscar Nitzchke and his project for the Maison de la Publicité; going as far, perhaps, as the New Babylon of Constant Nieuwenhuys.

These, however, are only brief, general references, and in sum they are of relatively limited value. What counts is that the elevation designed by the Piano and Rogers team was the total place of the effect and of the exteriorization, similar to many metropolitan spaces, where "the public finds itself in the pure external dimension and the disintegrated sequence of splendid sensory impressions brings reality to the fore," as Siegfried Kracauer had expressed it in 1926 (and in *Das Ornament der Masse*, 1963). Kracauer's book offers many

704,7

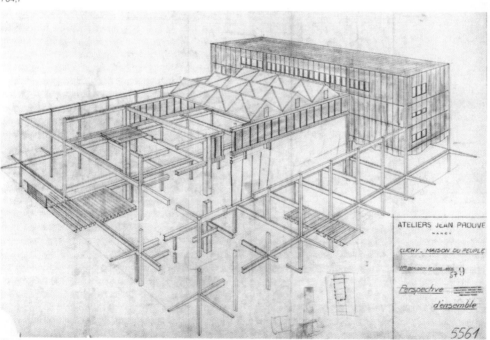

704,8

Oscar Nitzchke, Design for the Maison de la Publicité, Paris, c. 1932.

Constant Nieuwenhuys, *Ode à l'Odèon*, 1969.

Jean Prouvé, axonometric perspective of the Maison du Peuple, Clichy, 1939; designed by Eugène Beaudouin and Marcel Lods.

insights for evaluating a construction such as the Centre Pompidou and, more generally, "the painstaking magnificence of the exteriority," which is one of the main features of this building. Immersed in a directionless flow, encouraged to get their bearings without a compass through a geography formed by necessarily always-changing information, those who found themselves in front of or inside the building the architects originally conceived for Plateau Beaubourg could have been gratified by the spatial-temporal wanderings that mechanization permitted the masses to experience, stimulating the crowd's impulses and altering its configuration.

Instability and adaptability are the key features of the first project that, after 1974, was to become the Centre Georges Pompidou. The slabs of the floors, defined by a transparent wrapper or approached in terms of the 1936 drawings for Nitzchke's Maison de la Publicité, were to be mobile, preserving also from this point of view an echo of Cedric Price's Fun Palace. This proposal, which could never have been implemented in reality, as Silver notes, was nevertheless not discarded: in any case, expressed Rice, "it shows our attitude," as he imagined that its uncanny way of working could help to make the project's intentions clearer to the jury. Each level would have been free and open, the service spaces and technical equipment relegated to the edges, as in the Maison du Peuple of Clichy, built between 1935 and 1938 by Marcel Lods, Eugène Beaudouin, Jean Prouvé, and Vladimir Bodiansky. Even the vertical routes would not interrupt the continuous spaces. Having imagined the construction as a series of stacked warehouses, the initial decision—which was never challenged—was to create it with steel. The east and west elevations were punctuated by thirteen pillars, at intervals of 42 feet (12.8 meters), connected by slender St. Andrew's crosses. The columns would have been filled with water, providing protection in case of fire. The trusses, about 164 feet (50 meters) long, were of the Vierendeel type. There were three below-ground levels; a space of connection rose from the second, from which the staircases extended against the facade on the plaza, forking in a mannered way at the height of the second floor and continuing up to the fourth. The top floor was a roof garden. Since the internal spaces were not to be interrupted by supports, and the main girders were assigned the task of supporting the external circulation systems, the solution the architects envisioned for the competition project turned out to be too costly and invasive.

73   A Legitimate Transgression

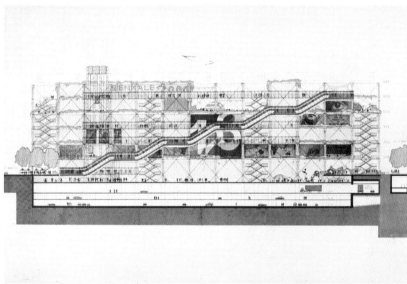

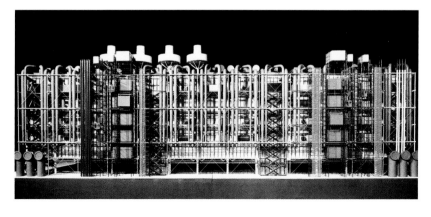

Renzo Piano, Richard Rogers, Gianfranco Franchini, Ove Arup & Partners, evolution of the competition design; the "jelly-mold scheme" and *avant-projet*, 1972, final model of the facade on the rue du Renard, c. 1975.

Complying with the contracted schedule, the group of designers submitted the *avant-projet sommaire* in March 1972. It satisfied Pompidou, but not the architects. The continuity between the plaza and the ground floor remained, but added in the levels above were a series of rounded joints, bringing to mind the Zip-Up House project of Richard and Su Rogers, and certain overhanging volumes that made the work very similar to "plug-in architecture." Rendered banal by a series of images that seem to have been borrowed from the pages of Archigram's fanzines, the presentation prompted the architects themselves to nickname it "the jelly-mold scheme." And one might say it seemed "moldy" as well—without the rugged clarity that marked the competition design. But the *avant-projet sommaire* does contain a decisive innovation, namely the abandonment of the Vierendeel trusses and the reduction of the spans. This rapidly led to the decision that gave the Centre Pompidou its definitive appearance.

The option chosen by the designers was to focus on the assembly of parts obtained by metal casting. In an attempt to be clear and persuasive, Piano and Rogers would explain that the Centre Pompidou had been constructed the way children build with toy construction sets, but this is an excessive, misleading, and even banal simplification. Instead, Rice explained, the goal he and the architects and engineers set out to achieve was to demonstrate to what extent "cast pieces can be refined by imagination." But even imagination, on its own, cannot explain how the building was constructed. The idea of using cast steel parts in fact came from multiple suggestions and it is not easy to map them reliably. Perhaps we can obviate a discussion of whether it is appropriate or not to include John Ruskin and William Morris—the nineteenth-century British fathers of the craft revival in design—among the ancestors of Centre Pompidou, as their legacy has been a way to frame the building in an older venerated tradition. Paris, and the buildings near to Plateau Beaubourg, already offered all the essential heritage for what Piano, Rogers, and Rice designed. But while the designers of the Centre Pompidou speak repeatedly, if in generic ways, about influence that the "capital of the nineteenth century"—the cradle of the art of construction that aims to "condense tensions in the most limited dimensions," as Sigfried Giedion observed—exercised on their work, we should pay attention to other forebears the team carefully considered and precisely recalled. Among

them are two nearly simultaneous works whose construction involved casting, with particularly successful results. The first is the Festival Plaza built for Expo '70 in Osaka, Japan. In this case, to install a transparent roof of 957 by 354 feet (291.6 by 108 meters) supported by six columns at a height of 98 feet (30 meters), weighing 4,400 tons (4,000 tonnes) and lifted fully assembled to its final position, Kenzo Tange and the engineers of Yoshikatsu Tsuboi Institute and of Kawaguchi & Engineers made use of cast spherical joints on which to connect multiple linear struts lying on different planes and originating from different quarters, ascribable to the legacy of Max Mengeringhausen and Buckminster Fuller's research and experiments. The second work is the roof of the stadium built in Munich for the 1972 Olympic Games. For this structure, Frei Otto (with Behnisch & Partner and Leonhardt, Andrä, and Partner) had cast the deflectors of the cables placed on the heads of the posts that supported the reticular saddle-shaped shells of the roof. Although these deflectors are certainly not Otto's most elegant construction details, the Munich stadium was not only an ideal aesthetic model for the Centre Pompidou's designers, it was also a practical suggestion. Those peculiar components of the structure built in Munich in fact had been made by the company Pohlig, a subcontractor of Krupp responsible for the construction of the stadium, which would soon be involved in the building of the Centre Pompidou.

The objectives of the project that took form after the presentation of the "jelly-mold scheme" led to the full development, though with significant omissions, of what had been envisioned ideally in the competition project. All the services for public circulation and fluids management were incorporated in the secondary outer skeleton. This solution implied extending the trusses outward by about 49 feet (15 meters) for a total span of 147 feet 6 inches (45 meters); these overhangs made it possible to create two cages that form the main elevations containing "everything" that might encumber or obstruct the internal floors. Since the height of the building, given the regulations in effect at the time in Paris, had to be limited to 137 feet 9½ inches (42 meters), the original idea of making the footprint of the construction part of the plaza was abandoned in order to obtain more square feet of protected spaces. This opened the way for one of the most brilliant solutions developed by the architects and the engineers, translated into the design of the sloping plaza that now gently conveys the public toward the main entrance and then to the escalators hanging in front of the facade. Again to limit the height, the maximum height of the individual floors was set at about 23 feet (7 meters), thus making it necessary to pay particular attention to the sizing of the main girders, which in the end have a length of about 147 feet (44.8 meters) and are able to support a weight of 794 tons (720 tonnes). Given their span, the distance between the center of gravity of the element under compression and that under tension becomes about 8 feet 2½ inches (2.5 meters), to contain the rise. Taking the sum of this thickness and that of the floor slabs, the free spaces below the beams have a height of about 13 feet (4 meters). This final limitation lies at the beginning of the configuration of the installed Warren girders; their design maximizes transparency for the visual plane and makes evident the tensions to which they are subjected. Observing them, it is easy to see the different sizes of the members subjected to compression, whose diameter is 17¾ inches (450 millimeters), as opposed to those under tension, with a diameter that varies from 8⅞ inches (225 millimeters) at the center to 6⅜ inches (160 millimeters). Since the main members are split and thus crossed and washed by light, the functions of every beam component are perfectly legible, as the designers intended, or are "speaking," as we might say. Without interrupting the continuity of the spaces, the Warren girders thus assign the forces that determine the task of gauging their dimensions. Not compelled to also produce a secondary "architectural effect," as Piano usually puts it, the girders convey the refined "structural simplicity": every detail, performing its individual function as a part of a process of scheduled assembly, contributes to the entire construction.

The elegance that distinguishes the main girders becomes even more evident in the elements that most directly display the tactile qualities that casting imparts to steel. One of the objectives that the designers of the Centre Pompidou explicitly pursued was the ability to achieve what Rice called "the primitive magic which steel seems to have lost," and of bringing out the skilled craftsmanship involved in the molding process. This explains why the Centre Pompidou is actually "a parody of the technological imaginary, a crafted object made by hand, piece by piece," as Piano and Rogers like to recall, whose production starts with the preparation of the master molds in wood, from which those for the casting are produced. Though it has grown almost boundlessly, becoming

Explanatory model of the building structure of the Centre Pompidou.

Sequentially mounting the Warren girders, the gerberettes, and the external tie beams.

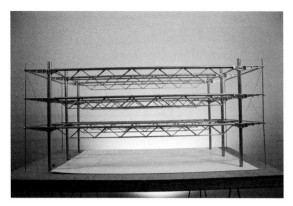

"gigantic," this "object" is therefore not so different from those Piano had designed before 1971, studying them using the models he built together with the craftsmen in his studio in Genoa, where the scent of wood mingled with that of resins.

Ultimately the key to the Centre Pompidou's "monstrous singularity" was in the refined conception of the Warren girders and the gerberettes—the forged steel pieces that connect the truss system to the vertical system, forming also the end connection with the St. Andrew's crosses and the vertical guys. This composition of different structural meanings, assembled following a strict and unchangeable procedure, generates the configurations of the two main facades, which convey the otherwise lost appeal of the material with which they were built and the unusual qualities of the work that went into their casting. But to understand the functioning of the gerberettes—carefully shaped prostheses that extend the main truss girders in an overhang and support the cages containing the

Lifting a gerberette.

Heinrich Gerber, bridge over the Main, Hassfurt, Germany, 1867.

Peter Rice, comparative analysis of bridge structures: (A) bridge with a single span: easily built but susceptible to uneconomical deformations; (B) bridge with continuous beam: difficult to build and susceptible to certain deformations; (C) Gerber beam: easy to build and susceptible to fewer potential deformations.

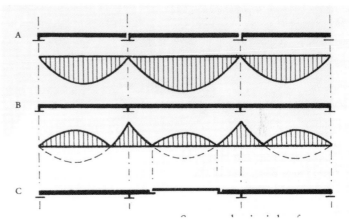

services—we need to once again take a short step back in time, to return to what Rice recalled as "my days in Sydney." That was where he "learned a key lesson," we read in *An Engineer Imagines*: "the importance of the integrity of the building's construction," and "the *gerberette* and the decision to use cast steel in the Centre Pompidou" come from this lesson.

The name of these unusual consoles, gerberettes, has prompted amusing associations, in the literature devoted to the Beaubourg, with the phonetically similar words *lorette*, *grisette*, and *cocotte*, names assigned to the ladies who inspired the erotic impulses in Haussmann's Parisian boulevards. Actually the term comes from the name of the German engineer Heinrich Gerber, a serious nineteenth-century servant of the state, famous for his iron bridges and the holder of a patent for the construction of hinged girders. Gerber invented the saddle that in the Centre Pompidou acquired, in his honor, the name gerberette. The Gerber saddle is a hinge; it does not transmit the bending moment (M=Fd) and does not permit longitudinal movements. In 1857, building the bridge on the Main at Hassfurt, Gerber had developed a console girder, or a continuous beam with strategically positioned hinges, that was based on the same system used in Friedrich August von Pauli's lenticular trusses that same year to build the bridge over the Isar at Grosshesselohe. Heinrich Gerber lived between 1832 and 1912, and when we look at the Centre Pompidou or discuss its construction techniques, it is worth considering the principle that states that the past never disappears from the present and the present is never free from the past—one of the meanings of the Italian expression *contemporaneità dell'inattuale*—what is outdated never ceases to reappear as the present, which is more than a simple warning for mainly historians of architecture.

The form of the gerberettes diagrams the stresses to which they are subjected. Each one, with a length of 27 feet (8.2 meters) and weighing 10.58 tons (9.6 tonnes), is the product of a single casting. The positions and configurations of the perforations that cross their volume offer a snapshot of the succession of the assembly phases. The largest parts, subjected to the greatest strains, have an accentuated ovoid profile and contain openings that permit their insertion on the columns that support them; the latter have a circular section with a diameter of about 2 feet 8 ³⁄₈ inches (85 centimeters); and, 137 feet 9 ⁵⁄₈ inches (42 meters) in height, they have thickness varying from 3 ³⁄₈ inches (85 millimeters) at the base to 1 ⁵⁄₈ inches (40 millimeters) at the end. To avoid subjecting them to eccentric loads, a spherical joint allows the gerberettes to rotate and bend without transferring moments to the columns. On the two sides of the gerberettes there are holes to accept the attachment joint, accommodating the longitudinal bracing. The slenderest portions protrude with sections that taper toward the end, where connection joints with the vertical ties are positioned. The heads of the terminations are attached to other joints, known as "sputniks": their position justifies the playful name, a tribute to the first artificial satellite in orbit around the earth, launched by the Soviet Union in 1957; the outermost braces are attached to these circular plates. The main trusses, on the other hand, are connected to the rotated openings that end the innermost portions, which are solid and smaller than the gerberettes, which function as a saddle. In this way the gerberettes are able to distribute the weight of the beams into forces of compression and tension. The compression is then transmitted to the columns, while the ties placed at the points of the greatest overhang cope

Centre Pompidou, connection between the Warren girder and a gerberette through the saddle.

Centre Pompidou, cross-section showing the connections between main beams, gerberettes, and columns.

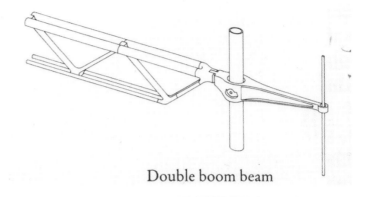

Double boom beam

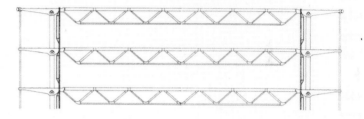

with the tension. The combinations, insertions, and overlays of these components—thick in the case of the gerberettes, drawn out in the case of the Warren girders, slender and of different diameters in the case of the ties—give the Centre Pompidou its form, starting from an intuition that Rice credits to his colleague Johnny Stanton, and in turn based on a structural connector developed by a nineteenth-century German engineer and an obsolete construction technique.

Such cast steel components were still produced in the 1970s, Rice recalled, "in foundries dating back to the mid-1800s, especially in the heart of the old European industrial system."

[In these foundries] the crafts methods and mentality had not changed much since the 1800s. We had to reconcile this tradition with today's requirements of reliability and analysis. A new technology was emerging at the time to respond to the need to produce reliable steel enclosures for nuclear reactors and to cope with the complexity of oil drilling platforms operating in the deep, cold waters of the North Sea. This technology was called fracture mechanics, a science that predicted the behavior of

83   A Legitimate Transgression

metals under stress and their reactions if there were small cracks or breaks inside. This seemed like the answer, so we worked with the institutes that focused on control of welding techniques in France and England to understand how to use this technology to forecast the behavior of the *gerberettes* and to decide what material should be used to make them.

After conducting progressive breakage trials on full-size samples to determine the ratios between stresses and deformations, the intensity of the critical stresses, and the ultimate strength, it was possible to decide which type of steel to use. This was followed by the production of the pieces: once cast, and after cleaning, the gerberettes were subjected to an initial thermal treatment, re-analyzed, given a second thermal treatment, and then load tested.

While this construction method was being developed, the evolution of the design and the increasing concerns related to costs led to abandoning certain solutions envisioned at the time of the competition. The use of stainless steel was reduced and the structure was painted to protect the joints from fire. The building gradually lost the appearance it would have had if it had truly been built as an "informative tool." The large, luminous screens that were supposed to dominate the plaza elevation on the west facade were replaced by a long escalator that crosses the facade in a broken diagonal red line where the spans are not occupied by the emergency staircases. The ramps mark the succession of the levels, making explicit the layout of the functions contained in the building and reordering the alternation of empty and full volumes in the upper part. They also allow the public to establish an empathetic and visual proximity with the tactile appeal of the structural details, with the escalators extending the experience of a mechanized architectural promenade. As in the case of the sloped plaza that comes before it, the glass enclosure around the ramps preserves the memory of the permeability that the Piano and Rogers team first envisioned when they prepared the competition project, and maintains the aspect of a "machine" that kept it from being simply a "container of art."

In the end, the plaza facade is marked by just one feature, the long staircase with its profile painted in red. It is to the east, in the elevation on rue du Renard, that the work bears the features of a complete and resolved composition. On rue du

Drawing of a gerberette with specifications for the steel, tolerances, and construction methods.

The production of the gerberettes in the Pohlig Heckel Bielchart factory, Krupp Group, in Rohrbach, Germany, 1974.

Renard, the gerberettes and ties stand out in all their apparent lightness. The vertical posts behind them vanish behind the succession of grouped conduits, clustered by color and size, which rise straight up and then bend over the roof crowded with the large circular ventilation ducts, the cooling towers, and the upper housings for the elevators. This is a true tour-de-force that owes much to Tom Barker, another engineer at Ove Arup & Partners, responsible for the form of the elevation emerging as an image of the order imposed by the throng of conduits that control the "environment" of the building.

While it is legitimate to think of the Centre Pompidou as a monument, this facade suggests that it was perhaps hasty to call it an "involuntary monument," as we did. The east facade brings out what is usually not visible; it is made with "minimal" and anonymous materials that are redeemed, as called for in the most radical application of the principles derived from "the spirit of lightness and economy," by a careful operation of assembly. This work can be associated with principles that—as architect Louis Kahn, who met Piano when he was working in Philadelphia with Robert Le Recolais, put it—"cost nothing": the correct proportions, the right relationships, the proper balances between served spaces and serving spaces did not add to the demands placed upon the budget. The elevation of the Centre Pompidou on rue du Renard is composed of colored volumes and lines whose design is dictated by the pattern of flows, from those of air to those represented by the movement of the elevators. These features are compressed and then juxtaposed, leaving nothing to chance: the lines are intensified, repeated, grouped, while the volumes have an unpredictable capacity to set the rhythm of the facade, incorporating movement inside it. This front that emerges from a narrow street is not concerned with appearances, but is designed in the coherent way its materials have been treated and its function expressed. The pressing succession of posts of surprising size that run from ground to roof illustrates the effort the building has to make to be able to offer its visitors, on the opposing front, the pleasing panorama seen from the staircase hung on the gerberettes and the view of the plaza and the vast open spaces to which the mobile ramps grant access. The rhetoric-free aesthetic of the facade on rue du Renard comes from abolishing the *chienlit*, the mask, from granting unabashed visibility to function and to all those things that, usually disguised or hidden, allow the space to take on its characteristics of usability.

Drawing of a Warren girder describing the specifications for the steel and tolerances.

Production of the Warren girders in the Krupp factories at Essen, Germany, 1974.

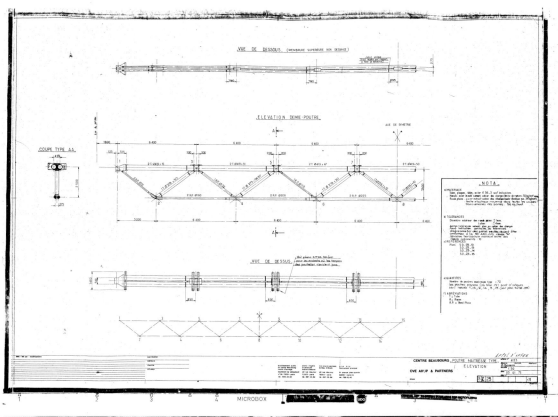

The uniqueness of the Centre Pompidou comes from the imagination and curiosity demonstrated by the designers who built it, treating proven methods in an experimental way, considering the obsolete and the new with the same objective detachment, aiming to surprise and reassure, only to realize during the course of the project that the content of a work and the inadvertent impulses it generates can shed light on and enhance each other. The elevations of the Centre Pompidou and, more precisely, the entire enclosure, possess disconcerting personalities. For those familiar with architecture, it is not hard to understand that the various planes of the ties attached at the heads of the gerberettes, the columns behind them, and the glass walls seem to indicate that they actually are an illusion. Each main facade, especially the one on rue du Renard, provides in fact a monoeclous apparatus. The parts that perform opposing static functions, under compression or under tension, form an organism shaped by a balancing game, the result of the intelligence with which the architects and engineers have managed to work together, designing the building "with rigor and discipline, piece by piece." Among the many details that can be observed in the Centre Pompidou, one in particular prompts an inevitable conclusion: the cast and forged node that connects each of the gerberettes to each column. Its form is the clearest demonstration that those who built the Centre Pompidou truly believed that the discussion, associated with architects and theorists such as Jean-Baptiste Rondelet from over a century earlier, over the difference between composition and construction had been laid to rest.

The saddle, the connection between the Warren girders and the gerberettes.

Chapter Five
The Intact Beauty of Paris

As much as 60 percent of the steel used for the construction of the Centre Pompidou's parts other than the expansion joints is cast steel. The first span was installed on October 31, 1974, and in April 1975 the work was complete. To avoid on-site welding as much as possible, the parts of the skeleton are remarkably large. Each of the columns, produced in France by the Société des Fonderies de Pont-à-Mousson, reached Paris in two sections. The main girders and the gerberettes, produced by Krupp and Pohlig, were transported in finished form from Germany; three of them reached the worksite each week. Before their assembly, teams of workmen, mostly from North Africa, erased the Krupp logo from each piece. Most of these workers were Algerian, and Nathan Silver is correct when he says that "Beaubourg was an Algerian achievement as much as a French and British-Italian one." Saying this, however, he neglected to mention that among the ancestors of the gerberettes is a bridge built at Hassfurt, in Bavaria, by a German engineer, and that like the Warren girders, they were cast in German foundries and made by German workers. These circumstances explain some of the tension with which French architectural culture, which tends to express itself in its native tongue, observed the construction of the Centre Pompidou, entrusted to designers speaking mostly English and Italian. Of course linguistic obstacles cannot account for the number of lawsuits confronted by those responsible for the construction of the Centre Pompidou—seven, Silver notes—more lawsuits than years that passed between the end of the competition and the opening on January 31, 1977. The motivations behind these lawsuits varied, as did those of the protests that accompanied the construction of the "huge machine" designed by Piano and Rogers. One of these stands out in particular, a good example due to the arguments advanced for it.

In the issue of February 14, 1972, *Le Nouvel Observateur* hosted an open letter from architect André Bergerioux that bitterly criticized an article signed by André Fermigier published in the same magazine three weeks earlier that focused on questions related to the construction at Plateau

Gustave Caillebotte, *Place de l'Europe*, 1877. Art Institute of Chicago.

Beaubourg. Bergerioux spoke in the name of the association *Geste architectural*, formed to emphasize, as we read in *Le Nouvel Observateur*, that "a work without a gesture is not an architectural work." In 1971 the jury chaired by Prouvé, having excluded the idea that their assigned task was to select from the projects submitted in the competition for Plateau Beaubourg the one most suited to the construction of a new monument, had also coherently and explicitly stated its lack of interest in proposals that would take the form of "architectural gestures." Given these premises, Bergerioux asserts, it is possible to explain how the "allergy to the architectural gesture" that seemed to afflict the jury had led to the choice of a project "focusing only on technique and programming" that had the goal to "enslave man to the machine." In the view of the spokesperson of *Geste architectural*, this unfortunate result was influenced by Prouvé, an engineer not an architect, who for this reason, he asserted, was therefore not only not suitable but also not qualified legitimately to take on the role of jury chairman. While Fermigier responded in kind, also from the pages of *Le Nouvel Observateur*, Bergerioux's letter can be seen as more than just an episode of folklore, though it does have those characteristics. Formulated in different terms, its accusation and scornful terminology—"huge machine"—would long accompany Centre Pompidou, along with the dark ghost of the razed Les Halles. Had Bergerioux simply been one of the many disappointed participants in the competition for Plateau Beaubourg there would have been little reason to heed his complaints. But Bergerioux in fact considered himself the defender of the ethics and the rights of the profession as practiced in France, whose praxis was being challenged by what was happening at Plateau Beaubourg.

The project by Piano, Rogers, Franchini, and Ove Arup & Partners, as we have seen, was developed by people who, unlike a certain professional class trained at the École des Beaux-Arts, did not consider "l'architecte comme l'homme de croquis" (the architect as the man of the sketch). Their creation was the result of a different culture, of the mentality of the architect-engineer, who considered practice as the basis of architecture. The huge machine had been conceived by them "piece by piece," as Joly did building Les Halles, which implied that every detail had been drawn and designed, and that the development of the building had been paced by the synchrony with which "innovation and creation" were combined in its parts. The construction solutions were defined in a "rigorous and disciplined way" together with the design. Only in this way could a building be raised that was built "to last not for 20 years, but for 300, 400, 500 years," thanks to its capacity to last by incessantly transforming, of finding its meaning also by adapting to the most radical events, even to "a new May 1968," as Piano concludes, with a phrase whose meaning cannot escape even those without a particular taste for psychoanalytic pastimes.

Bergerioux was one of many defenders of the traditional modes of organization of the architectural profession in France. Those working in the Paris studio of Piano and Rogers had noticed that in France "the architect is the person who goes home early" as Silver observed. Once the design was finished, Silver wittily reports, for a French architect the job could be considered done. In keeping with academic praxis, Rice observes, the design then is sent to the drafting department "which translates it into something more or less buildable. After this the contractor takes over, with the task of preparing the definitive drawings." This practice had not become established only to cope with postwar reconstruction for which Claudius-Petit had been the minister in charge, with Robert Bordaz as his right-hand man. Its origins can be traced back to the progressive evolution of the professional code outlined by Julien Guadet, which at the end of the 1800s had established, among other things, the incompatibility between the profession of the architect and the management of a business. This stipulation, which had created significant difficulties for Auguste Perret, the "failed student" of Guadet, and later with more dramatic implications for Fernand Pouillon, also indirectly explains the accusations advanced by the "architects of gesture" against Prouvé, not considering him suitable to chair the jury of the competition for Plateau Beaubourg.

Robert Bordaz was well aware of this situation and capable of grasping its implications. Having dealt also with Pouillon when the time came to intervene on the problematic reconstruction of the old port of Marseille after 1949, he knew how to maneuver around the situation and establish an arrangement with the designers of the Centre Pompidou that put them in a position of responsibility for every phase of the work, taking on tasks that according to French praxis were usually divided among the architect, the *bureau d'études*, and the contractor. During the first phases of the negotiations

ÉTABLISSEMENT PUBLIC
DU
Centre Beaubourg

Le 19 juin 1972

Monsieur Robert BORDAZ,   Conseiller d'Etat,
Président chargé de la Direction
de l'Etablissement Public du
Centre Beaubourg,

et

Monsieur Michel WEILL,   Architecte,
Secrétaire Général de l'Union
Internationale des Architectes,

tiennent à préciser les faits suivants concernant la person-
nalité de Monsieur Jean Prouvé et les conditions dans les-
quelles il a été appelé à présider le Jury du Centre Beaubourg.

1°) Si Monsieur Jean Prouvé ne s'est jamais présenté comme
architecte, il est par contre universellement reconnu comme
tel en raison de la qualité exceptionnelle de ses travaux
qui l'inscrivent déjà dans l'histoire de l'architecture
contemporaine.

Industriel jusqu'en 1950, ingénieur-conseil de nombreu-
ses entreprises, M. Jean Prouvé a participé (et participe
encore aujourd'hui) à la construction de nombreux bâtiments:
le CNIT, l'Institut Français des Pétroles, le Palais des
Congrès à Liège, l'aéroport d'Orly, la Tour Nobel à Puteaux,
l'Ecole d'Architecture de Nancy, etc... Il a joué et joue
encore un rôle fondamental dans la conception et la réalisation de nombreux prototypes originaux de constructions
industrielles.

Ingénieur au Conservatoire National des Arts et Métiers
jusqu'en 1963, M. Prouvé est actuellement Président du
Cercle d'Etudes Architecturales.

2°) Tous ceux qui le connaissent peuvent témoigner de la
droiture scrupuleuse de Monsieur Jean Prouvé.

230 J 27

2

3°) Il est exact que Monsieur Jean Prouvé a été un défenseur
convaincu des Pavillons de Baltard. La seule communication
écrite à ce sujet consiste en un article d'environ 20 lignes.
Mis à part cet article, il n'est l'auteur d'aucun ouvrage ni
d'aucun projet sur la rénovation du Centre de Paris, ou d'aucun projet de construction (même réduit à de simples suggestions). analogue au projet lauréat.

4°) Monsieur Jean Prouvé, sans être candidat, a été élu Président du Jury. Il ne l'avait pas demandé. Il ne s'y atten-
dait pas.

5°) On ne peut admettre l'affirmation selon laquelle Monsieur
Jean Prouvé "auteur du Projet, serait fournisseur de maté-
riel".

  Messieurs Robert Bordaz et Michel Weill ne peuvent que
regretter que Monsieur Jean Prouvé soit l'objet d'aussi vai-
nes et basses attaques.

something changed, however, in the relationship between the
designers and Bordaz: Ove Arup & Partners did not accept
the conditions outlined in the agreements and thought it was
not prudent to assume the risks that Piano and Rogers, on
the other hand, were willing to take. Though the engineers
of Structure 3 thus became merely consultants to the studio
of Piano and Rogers, the quality and importance of their
contribution to the project did not significantly change.

The controversy triggered by Bergerioux was not an
isolated incident. In less ingenuous ways, contention was
also fueled by others, including for example *L'Architecture
d'aujourd'hui*, which in issue 189 (1977) invited a number
of architects to publicly express their views on the recently
opened Centre Pompidou. On this occasion Peter Cook, while
praising Piano and Rogers, could not refrain from emphasizing that the Centre Pompidou "comes after" the Fun Palace
and Archigram, of which he was one of the founders. Peter
Smithson admitted that he admired the construction, but
with a certain touch of English malice he associated it with
the "rhétorique gauloise." Of the group, Rob Krier was the

most explicit: "Never before has a building prompted in me such violent physical discomfort." The most interesting pages of this issue of the magazine, though, are those containing an interview conducted with Prouvé by Hélène Demoraine. Demoraine does her best to get Prouvé to admit what she sees as his responsibilities for the results of the competition and the making of the work. "Do you feel responsible for the Centre Pompidou?" she asks as the first question. Prouvé not sharing, she asks—using chauvinistic arguments often present in the reactions the Centre Pompidou stimulated in France—about the discomfort felt by Parisians faced by the "foreign spot" that has taken form in the center of Paris, given the fact that "the architects are English and Italian, the consultant, Ove Arup, is English, and Krupp is the supplier of the beams?" "In short," she concludes, "you have never regretted the choices made by the jury?" Prouvé's answer is blunt: "Jamais" (never).

To understand the meaning of this reply, it is worth remembering the relations that connected Prouvé to the designers of Centre Pompidou. "Jean Prouvé came into my life in the moment in which we were developing the Centre Pompidou project, prior to the start of construction," Rice wrote in 1990. "His enthusiastic support made a big contribution to reinforce our conviction that it was possible to make metal carpentry as we had designed it, in spite of the general opposition of the world of French engineers and contractors." Piano recalled that "he often talked about automobiles and airplanes . . . [and] because I was doing research on light structures, we had very absorbing discussions. Working on lightness means studying the concentration of forces and therefore discovering the universe. *Jean Prouvé est un morceau de ma vie* [Jean Prouvé is a part of my life]."

Setting aside these memories and controversies that have accompanied the building's existence, if we want to delve into the more justified criticisms of the Centre Pompidou we need not return to those advanced by observers who, even today, may see it as a depressing reminder of lost battles, from the struggle to preserve Les Halles to the workings of the French architectural profession. We do better to go back to what Prouvé himself wrote, with a certain amount of coquetry defining himself: "I am only a worker." He referred to the fact that he was no stranger to work at the forge; when he was eighteen years old he was an apprentice first to the ironworker Émile Robert in Enghiem, and later in the workshop of Adalbert

Szabo. Prouvé, in other words, was a *forgeon serrurier* (black-smith), as had been Pierre-François Joly, the builder of Les Halles. The support and advice he gave to the designers of the gerberettes thus were valuable because they were founded in an exceptional experience and knowledge. For the same reasons, it is not surprising that his most warm appreciation of the Centre Pompidou was followed by the most radical criticism of choices made by the architects and the engineers, a final demonstration of the freedom and integrity behind his judgment as chairman of the jury of the Plateau Beaubourg competition: "I followed the construction of Beaubourg and Piano became my friend," Prouvé said in 1983, "but if I had built it, I would have made Beaubourg a different way. Piano and Rogers insisted on producing the pieces in the foundry, while I would have used laminated parts, and I would have made more extensive use of welding. But for me Beaubourg remains a courageous building, the only one in recent years."

Prouvé aside, blame and responsibility continued to be assigned to the Centre Pompidou, while overlooking the true essence of the building. It is for these reasons too that, almost inevitably, the Centre Pompidou is seen in relation to the Eiffel Tower. This is not just because the parallel is fostered by what Giedion wrote in 1928 in *Bauen in Frankreich, Bauen in Eisen, Bauen in Eisenbeton* (*Building in France, Building in Iron, Building in Ferroconcrete*), talking about steel that "opens space, . . . reduces walls to transparent skin," fusing together the "muscles and skeleton" of constructions. What we have in mind are comparisons that go beyond what Meyer, Giedion, and Benjamin understood when speaking of iron architecture of the nineteenth century; these writers do not focus on what buildings are, but on how they appear and how they are used, and to a great extent they judge the buildings on use. Examples are found in comments by Marc Fumaroli and Giorgio Agamben, observers with whom we in most other matters agree. "The great secret of the Centre Pompidou is not its collection of works by Matisse, Picasso, Braque, Bonnard, but that escalator highlighted by a bright red railing," we read in *L'État culturel*. "Thanks to it, the tourist overlooks an admirable panorama over the rooftops of old Paris, and the photographer has a thousand opportunities, as on the different levels of the Eiffel Tower, to take lovely souvenir snapshots," continued Fumaroli, while Agamben added that the Eiffel Tower "transforms the whole city into merchandise that can be consumed in a single glance." Of course all this is partially true, but it is no less true that it is not enough to judge a building starting with the behavior of its users. By doing so, after all, one is often led to grant excessive space to nostalgia.

Also, if it is an exercise of intellectual indolence to link the Eiffel Tower and Centre Pompidou, this comparison is enhanced by the tendency any historian should avoid to reduce the interpretation of the present to semblances of the past. Mentioning an amusing event which took place during the construction of Centre Pompidou we can explain this point. While they were engaged in the construction of the center, Piano and Rogers received a forceful letter of protest signed by a number of architects. It was a prank, since the text very probably was based on an announcement that appeared about 90 years before in *Le Temps* on February 14, 1887. This original document, which had not been a prank, was entitled "Protestation des artistes," and its target was the Eiffel Tower. "We writers, painters, sculptors, architects," we read in *Le Temps*, "passionate lovers of the until-now intact beauty of Paris, protest with all our strength and all our indignation in the name of offended French taste, in the name of threatened French art and history, against the useless and monstrous construction of the Eiffel Tower. Without any chauvinistic excess, we have the right to boldly state that Paris is a city without rivals in the world." The signatures of Léon Bonnat, William Bouguereau, Ernest Meissonier, François Coppée, Alexandre Dumas fils, Guy de Maupassant, Éduard Pailleron, Victorien Sardou, Charles Garnier, Charles Gounod, and Eugène Guillaume accompanied this statement, which can only be defined as stentorian. The self-absolution from any suspicion of chauvinism on the part of the authors deserves only passing attention—*Excusatio non petita, accusatio manifesta* (He who excuses himself, accuses himself). What is more striking is that the same arguments are still current today. The previously mentioned interview conducted by Hélène Demoraine with Jean Prouvé published in 1977 in *L'Architecture d'aujourd'hui* is small proof of this. This minor proof, in fact, can also be traced back to the passage in which, in the 1887 "Protestation," the authors speak of the "until-now intact beauty of Paris." Such a statement prompts us to ask not only what the distinguished men who signed the "Protestation des artistes" meant, but above all what they saw and how they saw Paris in 1887. It is true the defeat inflicted by Prussia on France in 1870 that produced the end of the

Gustave Eiffel, at center, at the foot of the Eiffel Tower, next to the "Appareil de Chute," which measured the resistance of falling objects, c. 1908.

empire "was perhaps a blessing for the architectural image of Paris, since Napoleon III," as Benjamin wrote, referring to the reforms carried out by Haussmann "intended to transform entire districts of the city." But Paris in 1887 was not the repository of "an until-now intact beauty" unless we inexplicably dismiss "the utterly arbitrary axes of Haussmann," as Le Corbusier called them, using a synecdoche, as unimportant urban planning transformations, nothing more than "financial and military measures," when they had in fact definitively altered the form, appearance, and nature of the city.

    Like the Eiffel Tower in the nineteenth century, less than one hundred years later the Centre Pompidou has been seen as a violation of the "intact beauty of a city that has no rivals"—but to make of Paris a city that has no rivals was precisely Pompidou's goal in building Beaubourg. Those who still believe that the Centre Pompidou violates Paris's past have probably given only a cursory reading to *Dicta and Contradicta* by Karl Kraus. Perhaps had Beaubourg been built as Piano, Rogers, and their team had envisioned in 1971, the huge screens they proposed to put on the main facade could have displayed for the inhabitants of the city and the visitors who nostalgically think of Paris as the homeland of an intact beauty, two lines from that book. Adjusted from Kraus's focus on his city, Vienna, they conserve their original, witty timeliness: "I have devastating news for the aesthetes: Old Paris was once new."

Entry for Plateau Beaubourg competition, 1971, the main facade.

L'outil informatif.

Portfolio of Photographs
and Drawings

< Centre Georges Pompidou seen from
the rue de Cloître Saint-Merri, facade
toward Place Georges Pompidou.

Plateau Beaubourg in the 1960s.

The excavation of Plateau Beaubourg
in 1975.

The production of the gerberettes in the
Pohlig Heckel Bielchart factory, Krupp
Group, in Rohrbach, 1974.

Warren girders in the Krupp factories
at Essen, 1974.

Lifting an overturned Warren girder,
c. 1975.

The gerberettes and the floor structure.

Construction of a floor.

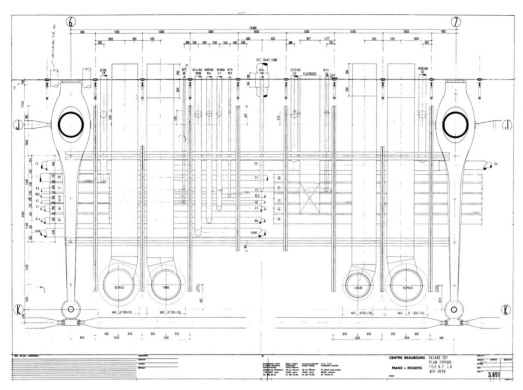

Finishing work on the west facade, 1976
(with the "sputnik" in the foreground).

Elevation drawing of the west facade showing the superimposed layers of the structure.

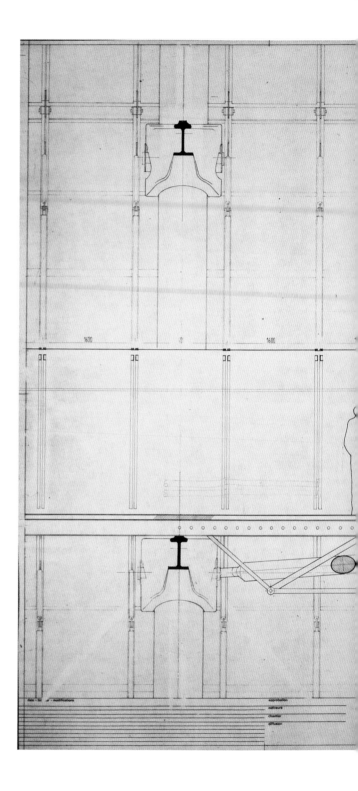

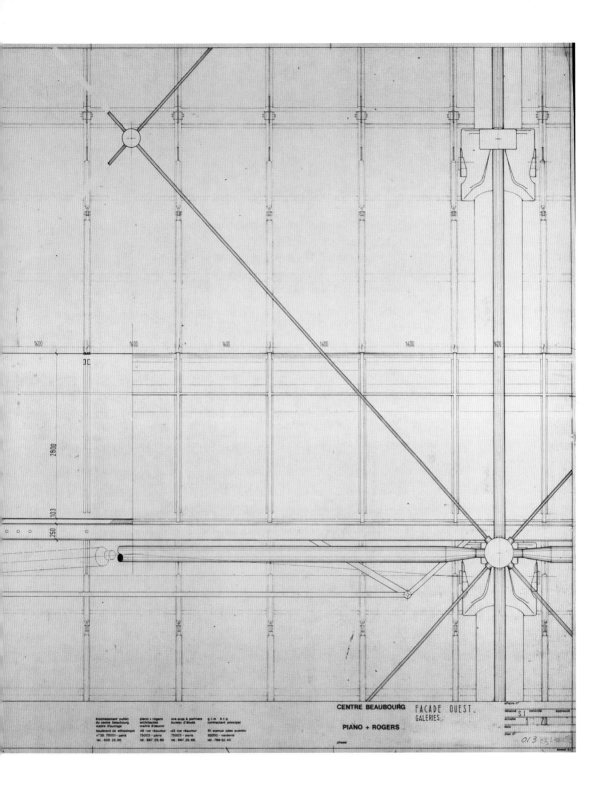

1600   1600   1600   1600   1600   1600

2800

103

250

CENTRE BEAUBOURG   FACADE OUEST.
                     GALERIES

PIANO + ROGERS

établissement public   piano + rogers   ove arup & partners   g.t.m b.t.p
du centre beaubourg   architectes   bureau d'étude   contractant principal
maître d'ouvrage   maître d'oeuvre
boulevard de sébastopol   49 rue réaumur   49 rue réaumur   61 avenue jules quentin
n°35 75001 - paris   75003 - paris   75003 - paris   92000 - nanterre
tél. 508 28.00   tél. 887.29.69   tél. 887.26.69   tél. 769 62 40

phase

013

Building Beaubourg.

Node with cross-bracing beams.

Drawing of the connecting pinions used for cross-bracing with the main beams.

Drawing of the pinion-type brace being inserted into the external end of the gerberette.

> The "sputnik" and the gerberette.

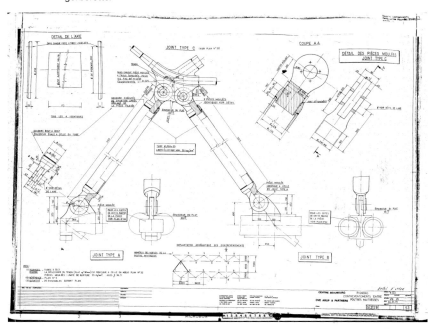

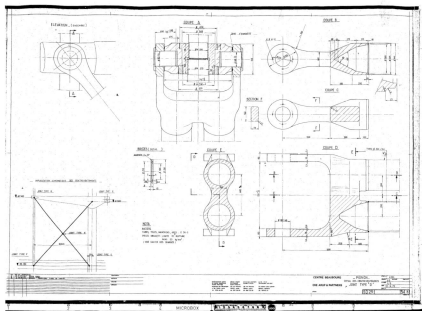

The nearly completed structure of
the building seen from the IRCAM
(Institut de Recherche et Coordination
Acoustique/Musique) construction
site, 1975.

The completed Centre Pompidou,
seen from above, with the area
formerly occupied by Les Halles
in the background.

Section drawing.

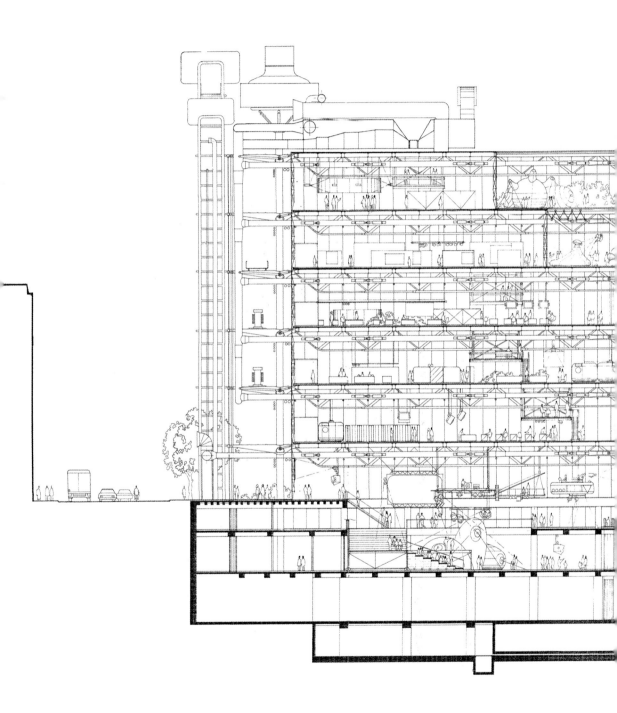

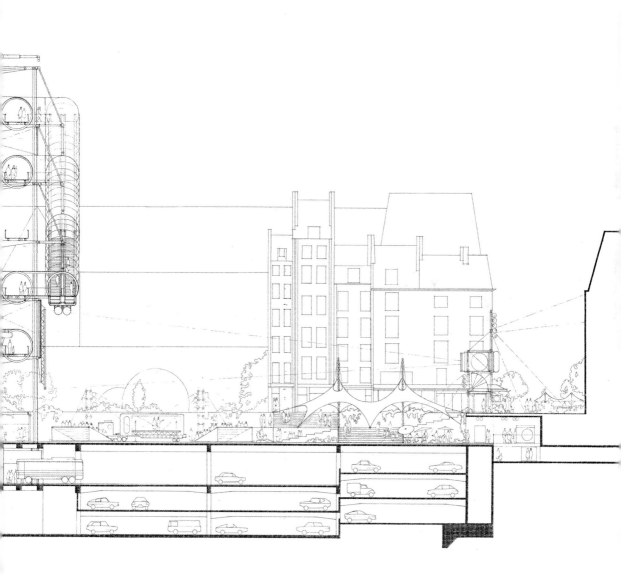

Partial view of the Centre Pompidou,
facing the Place Georges Pompidou.

Partial view of the external mobile
staircase (overlooking the Place
Georges Pompidou).

Partial views of the external mobile staircase (overlooking the Place Georges Pompidou).

Partial view of the external mobile staircase (overlooking the Place Georges Pompidou).

Explanatory drawing of the suspension
system of the external corridor and
mobile staircase.

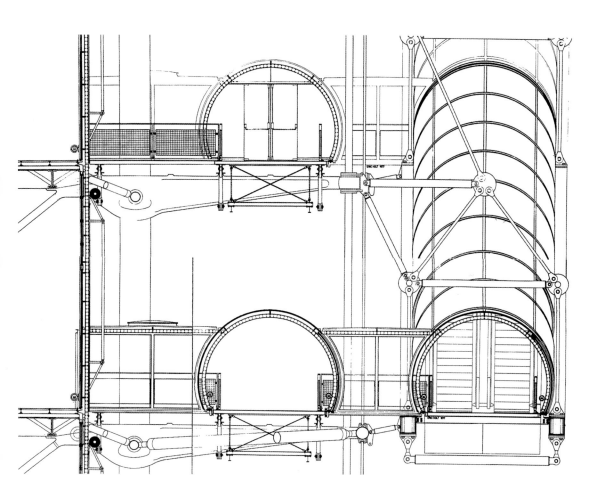

Facade on rue du Renard. Each color stands for a particular function: blue for ventilation, green for water, red for automated elevators, yellow for electricity. The main structure is white. Service structures (service stairs, passageways, etc.) are gray.

Facade on rue du Renard.

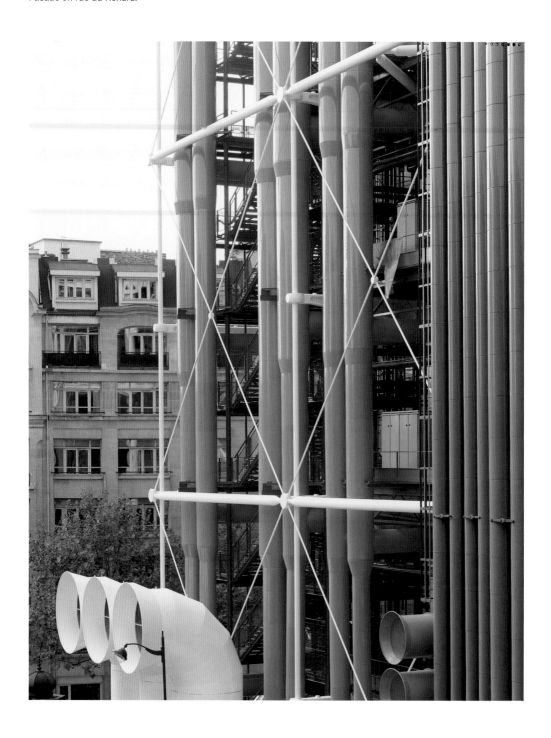

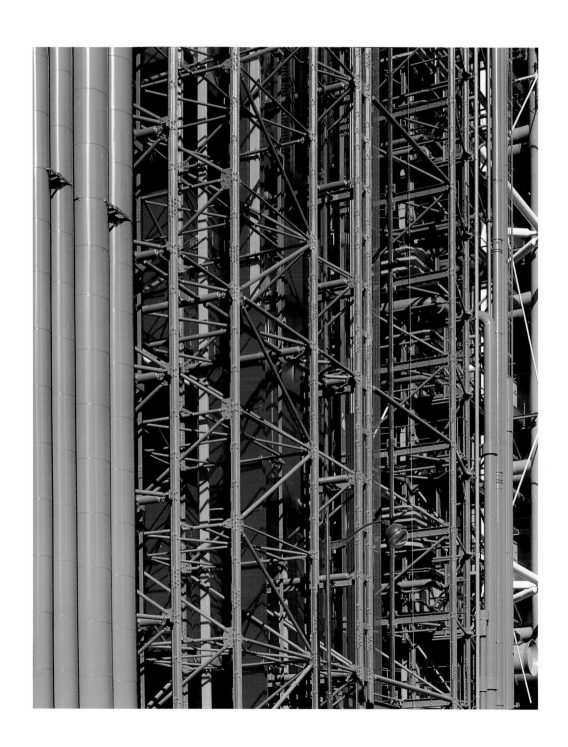

Explanatory drawing of the
air-conditioning duct system.

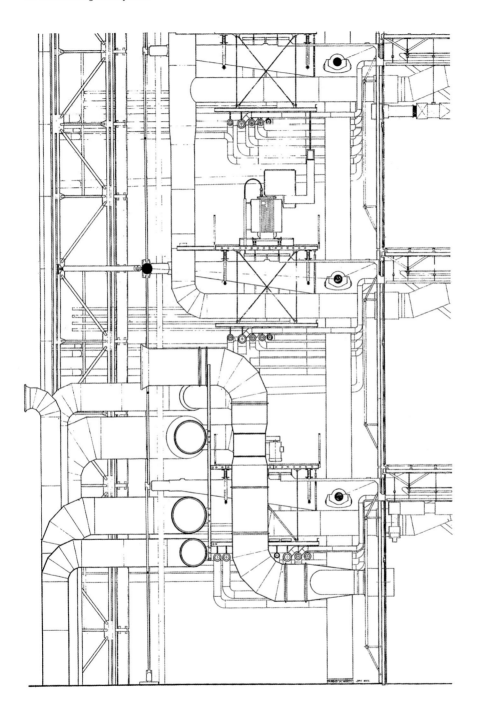

Facade toward the Fontaine
Stravinsky and IRCAM.

The covered square.

The museum space.

The library.

Outdoor exhibition space.

Place Georges Pompidou.

View from the top of the
Church of Saint-Merri.

Place Georges Pompidou.   > Aerial view.

The "sputnik."

Ventilation pipes in the Place Georges Pompidou, seen from the interior of the Centre.

View from the Fontaine Stravinsky.

Facade on rue du Renard.

Bibliographical Note

In writing this book I have considered as "fellow-workers" (Virginia Woolf's expression, which I cited in the preface) the many authors and their numerous books dedicated to the Centre Georges Pompidou that came before me. I think it is appropriate to acknowledge them here and explain the extent to which I have relied on them. In so doing I also hope to supply the reader with some helpful information.

I became familiar with the history of the Centre Georges Pompidou thanks to Nathan Silver's book *The Making of Beaubourg* (1994). The book is accurate, informed, and includes a helpful appendix. In addition to Silver's book, even if they do not always provide original information, I also kept in mind the following: I. Zaknic, *Pompidou Center* (1983); R. Piano and R. Rogers, *Du Plateau Beaubourg au Centre Georges Pompidou* (1987); G. Denti, *R. Piano, R. Rogers, O. Arup: Il Centre Georges Pompidou* (1998); J. L. Cohen and M. Eleb, "Centre Georges Pompidou," in J. L. Cohen and M. Eleb, *Paris: Architecture, 1900–2000* (2000); F. B. Dufrêne, *La Creation de Beaubourg* (2000); G. Ausiello and F. Polverino, *Renzo Piano: Architettura e tecnica* (2004); and G. Viatte, *Le Centre Pompidou: Les années Beaubourg* (2007).

Numerous articles appeared in specialized journals and the general press during the years the Centre Pompidou was being built and immediately after its opening in 1977. Among these, I paid particular attention to issue number 189 of *L'Architecture d'aujourd'hui* (February 1977), not only for its prestige and the fact that the issue was published immediately after the building's opening but also because it contains a chronology of the project, descriptions of the building's functions, writings by Renzo Piano and Richard Rogers ("L'Histoire du projet") and by Peter Rice ("La Structure metallique"), an eloquent interview with J. Prouvé by H. Demoriane, and a feature titled "La Parole est aux architects" that gathers the rancorous, critical, or reticent opinions of P. Cook, P. Smithson, R. Bofill, R. Krier, E. Aillaud, and G. Candilis. This issue of *L'Architecture d'aujourd'hui* is essential, and I recommend it to readers. Two other issues of that journal, numbers 168 and 170 from 1973, also contain ample references to the project for Beaubourg and to Piano and Rogers. Other journal volumes that I consulted include *Domus* 525 (August 1973); *Architectural Design* 5 (May 1975); *A+U* 66 (1976); *Bauwelt* 11 (March 1977); *Werk-Archithese* 9 (September 1977); *Domus* 575 (October 1977); and *Bauen+Wohnen* 4 (1977); and if for nothing else than the title used in presenting the building, "The Pompodolium," *Architectural Review* 963 (May 1977).

In the book, I looked back on an episode that, along with number 189 of *L'Architecture d'aujourd'hui*, helps explain the spectrum of reactions that the construction of the Centre Pompidou aroused in France, particularly in the world of architecture. It concerns the stance taken by André Bergerioux, president of the association Geste Architectural, recorded and analyzed in the February 14, 1972, issue of *Le Nouvel Observateur*, which heralded the mounting reservations about Centre Pompidou expressed in 1977. Jean Prouvé did not fail to notice the controversy triggered by Bergerioux when speaking of his experience as chairman of the jury for the Beaubourg competition, which I have touched on in the book and will return to below. Lastly, among the numerous cinematographic documents dedicated to Beaubourg, still a moving tribute is *Le Centre Georges Pompidou* (54 minutes), the last film directed by Roberto Rossellini, created three months after the building opened in 1977.

Among the readings that I found most helpful in interpreting the significance of the Centre Pompidou are J. Baudrillard, "The Beaubourg Effect: Implosion and Difference," in *Simulacra and Simulation* (1994); also the comment on this source in *Rethinking Architecture*, edited by N. Leach (1997); and L. Pinto, "Déconstruire Beaubourg: Art, politique et architecture," in *Genèses* 6 (December 1991). M. Fumaroli's *L'État culturel: Essai sur une religion moderne* (1991), beyond its succinct observations relevant to the Centre Pompidou, provides a general framework of cultural politics in twentieth-century France that I found particularly well defined. Equally stimulating is Fumaroli's *Paris–New York et retour* (2009), which addresses the issue of cultural rivalries between the two cities, and of which the Centre Pompidou was one of the consequences. In writing about the Centre Pompidou as a museum, it was natural for me to consult two books by J. Clair along with those of Fumaroli: *Considérations sur l'état des beaux-arts* (1983) and *Malaise dans le musées* (2007).

In considering the construction of the Centre Pompidou within the context of Paris's urban planning, I turned to A. Fermigier's *La Bataille de Paris: Des Halles à la Pyramide* (1991). This book gathers what was written by Fermigier (the protagonist of the controversy with Bergerioux) about Paris's urban transformations, first in *Le Nouvel Observateur* and then in *Le Monde*. This book thus allowed me to understand the positions of the most important voices of French public opinion about events closely tied to those leading to the construction of the Centre Pompidou. Even though it is not directly related to the Centre Pompidou, I also used F. Fromonot, *La Campagne des Halles* (2005), because it sheds light on consequences that derived from the destruction of Les Halles. To this end, concerned with the history of Les Halles, I relied on B. Lemoine, *Les Halles de Paris* (1980), which includes comprehensive documentation and the facsimile reproduction of V. Baltard and F. Callet's *Monographie des Halles Centrales* (1863). As for the urban interventions made in Paris by Georges Haussmann under Napoleon III, including the construction of Les Halles, the literature is vast. A good bibliographic account can be found in the catalogue by J. Des Cars and P. Pinon, *Paris–Haussmann, le pari d'Haussmann* (1991), published on the occasion of a beautiful exhibition of the same name held that year at the Pavillion de l'Arsenale in Paris.

As the reader may have gathered, all that I have written about Paris stems from a way of observing, knowing, and loving the city that I learned from the writings of Walter Benjamin. Though perhaps an exaggeration, every page of this book, either directly or indirectly, owes a debt to *The Arcades Project* (*Das Passagenwerk*, 1982). Reading the writings of Benjamin in general carries the consequence of reading many other books; among these are three that I was particularly drawn to: L. Aragon, *Nightwalker* (*Le Paysan de Paris*, 1926; 1970); A. G. Meyer, *Eisenbauten, ihre Geschichte und Æsthetik* (1907); S. Giedion, *Building in France, Building in Iron, Building in Ferroconcrete* (*Bauen in Frankreich, Bauen in Eisen, Bauen in Eisenbeton*, 1928; 1995). The writings of Meyer and Giedion in particular were fundamental to some of the conclusions I have drawn about the evolution of statics and engineering solutions in light of those adopted by the designers of the Centre Pompidou. In this case I used the collected volume edited by A. Picon, *L'Art de l'ingénieur* (1997); the studies of T. Peters, *Building the Nineteenth Century* (1996);

that of M. Wells, *Engineers: A History of Engineering and Structural Design* (2010); portions of K-E. Kurrer, *The History of the Theory of Structure* (2008); and B. N. Sandaker, A. P. Eggen, and M. R. Cruveller, *The Structural Basis of Architecture* (1992).

For understanding the 1971 decision to hold a competition for the construction of what was then called Centre Beaubourg, I considered it essential to pay particular attention to the jury charged with carrying out the task. The members of the jury are so well known, however, that it would be superfluous to provide additional sources on them now—with the exception of Jean Prouvé. His life and work have been studied by P. Sulzer, author of *Jean Prouvé: Oeuvre complète* (4 vols., 1995–2008). A satisfactory account, accompanied by interesting historiographic insights, was given to me in the Centre Pompidou catalogue *Jean Prouvé constructeur* (1990); Renzo Piano was among those responsible for organizing the exhibition accompanying this publication, and included in the catalogue are an interview with Piano, for whom Prouvé "was more than a friend," and Peter Rice's brief essay "L'Ingénieur." I found elements of notable interest regarding the competition for the Centre Beaubourg, accompanied by a fundamental critique of the work's conception as realized, in the small but invaluable book edited by A. Lavalou, *Jean Prouvé par lui-même* (2001). I paused briefly in the book to discuss the Maison du Peuple in Clichy (1937–39), which Prouvé built with M. Beaudin and M. Lods; I suggest it would be wise for curious readers to consider this work carefully. In addition to the books written on Prouvé and on Lods and in the few journals concerned with their work at the time, I relied on B. Simonot's small publication *La Maison du Peuple de Clichy-la-Garenne* (2010). In reading what Simonot wrote, I came across a quote taken from a speech made by Prouvé in 1950 at the Société des Ingénieurs-Soudeurs. I was not able to identify its source, but it was important in leading me to interpret the term *chienlit* as I did at the beginning of the book: Prouvé spoke about the need for architects to employ "modern technology" "sans camouflage, sans mensogne, sans tromperie" (without camouflage, without lies, without deception).

It is difficult to explain a project such as the one developed for Beaubourg without taking into account what happened in London during the 1960s and the cultural climate and atmosphere that young architects like Piano and

Rogers and engineers like Peter Rice and his colleagues at Ove Arup & Partners shared. Helping me to outline a framework of the times and the people were the books of J. Osborne, *Look Back in Anger* (1957); D. Sandbrook, *I Never Had It So Good: A History of Britain from Suez to the Beatles* (2005), and *White Heat: A History of Britain in the Swinging Sixties* (2006); D. Flower, *Youth Culture in Modern Britain* (2008); A. Sinfield, *Literature, Politics and Culture in Postwar Britain* (1989); and Michelangelo Antonioni's film *Blow-Up* (1966), especially eloquent for those who like me are compatriots of Piano. As regards the architectural culture, England of this period had Reyner Banham as its chosen interpreter. N. Whitely, in *Reyner Banham: Historian of the Immediate Future* (2002), carefully analyzed the life and contributions of this brilliant scholar. Without Banham's books *Theory and Design in the First Machine Age* (1960) and *The New Brutalism* (1966) and his numerous writings in diverse journals, I believe it would have been difficult to orient myself with what was flourishing in the English architectural culture of the 1960s. In his essays Banham treated some of the issues, both general and specific, that I confronted in this book, concentrating on figures and groups such as Cedric Price, James Stirling, and Archigram, and of course the Centre Pompidou. Banham's writings are collected in *A Critic Writes: Essays by Reyner Banham*, edited by M. Banham et al. (1966), and in *Architettura della seconda età della macchina*, edited by M. Biraghi (2004). Although it is best not to miss any of Banham's writings, I mention here the essays that I found particularly helpful: "Revenge of the Picturesque: English Architectural Polemics 1945–1965," in *Concerning Architecture*, edited by J. Summerson (1968); "Peoples' Palaces," *New Statesman* (August 7, 1964); "A Clip-on Architecture," *Architectural Design* (November 1965); and "Centre Pompidou," *Architectural Review* 161 (May 1977).

In treating Cedric Price, I read S. Matthews, *From Agit-prop to Free Space: The Architecture of Cedric Price* (2007), which contains ample bibliographic information, and C. Price, *Re: CP*, edited by H. U. Obrist (2003), in addition to the Architectural Association catalogue *Cedric Price* (1984). I became acquainted with Joan Littlewood thanks to her book titled *Joan's Book: Joan Littlewood's Peculiar History as She Tells It* (1995) along with that edited by E. MacColl and H. Goorney, *Agit-prop to Theatre Workshop: Political Playscripts*

1930–1950 (1986). For Archigram, I used the book by S. Sadler, *Archigram: Architecture without Architecture* (2005), which is accompanied by a bibliography that I imagine will be appreciated by those interested in learning more about this characteristic facet of English culture in the 1960s. Also on this topic, I consulted the Centre Pompidou exhibition catalogue *Archigram* (1994).

Based on what Banham wrote in *Theory and Design in the First Machine Age* and what is evident in reading what Piano and Rogers have said and done, I found it necessary to devote some attention to the works and writings of Buckminster Fuller. To learn about the design elements of his multifaceted work, I relied above all else on the four volumes edited by J. Ward, *The Artifacts of R. Buckminster Fuller* (1985). I became acquainted with the different aspects of his personality by consulting *The Buckminster Fuller Reader*, edited by J. Meller (1972); B. Fuller with K. Kuromiya, *Critical Path* (1981); and B. Fuller and K. Kuromiya, *Cosmography: A Posthumous Scenario for the Future of Humanity* (1991). Also useful were the Whitney Museum of American Art catalogue by K. M. Hays and D. Miller, *Buckminster Fuller* (2008), with its interesting essays; and for a somewhat different focus, L. Lorance, *Becoming Bucky Fuller* (2009).

The present book opens by discussing what happened in Paris in May 1968. The literature on this historic moment is vast and diverse. I have chosen to focus on information explaining why and how Georges Pompidou reached the decision to build Beaubourg. As introductions to these themes I used J. Foccart's *Foccart parle: Entretiens avec Philippe Gaillard* (1997) and E. Roussel's *Georges Pompidou* (2004). In addition, regarding the events of May 1968, I have relied on information from A. Touraine, *Le Communisme utopique: Le mouvement de Mai 1968* (1968); H. Hamon and P. Rotman, *Génération: Les années de rêve* (1987); K. Ross, *Mai 68 et ses vies ultérieures* (reprint 2010); V. Cespedes, *Mai 68: La philosophie est dans la rue* (2008); and finally R. Merle's novel, *Derrière le vitre* (1970).

I devoted particular attention to Robert Bordaz, president of the Établissement Public created for the construction of Centre Beaubourg, whose personality emerges from his personal history and his books: *Le Centre Pompidou: Une nouvelle culture* (1977) and *Pour donner à voir* (1987), with a preface by P. Boulez and the transcription of a conversation with Piano. But see also *Entretiens: Robert Bordaz, Renzo Piano* (1997) and the article "Centre national d'Art Georges Pompidou" in *Construction* 9 (1974). It is worth noting that one of the sources I used in writing about the Sydney Opera House and Peter Rice's contribution to the design of the Centre Pompidou, even if it is not among the most important, was R. Bordaz, "L'Opéra de Sydney," in *La Nouvelle Revue des deux mondes* (May 1972). An oral interview with R. Bordaz of particular interest is preserved by the Association Georges Pompidou in Paris. The interview is one of 179 collected by the association, issued by leading figures in French political, cultural, entrepreneurial, and financial life relating to the work of Georges Pompidou. In consulting this archive I obtained useful information relating to the events of May 1968 and leading to the construction of Centre Pompidou.

For Renzo Piano and Richard Rogers, a bibliography could become repetitive. Since the late 1970s many publications have been dedicated to their work, of which few stand out for their acumen and many offer a more or less complete catalogue of works as their principal merit. P. Buchanan has published *Renzo Piano Building Workshop*, now comprising five volumes (1999–2008). Among the books written by Piano, I paid particular attention to *Giornale di bordo* (in collaboration with R. Berignolo) (1977 and 2005), where he speaks at length about the construction of Centre Pompidou. Piano's *La responsabilità dell'architetto: Conversazione con Renzo Cassigoli* (2000) offers numerous insights into his work and helped me comprehend his intellectual journey in the years in which he published *Antico è bello: Il recupero della città* (with M. Arduino and M. Fazio, 1970) and *Dialoghi di cantiere* (1986). In discussing Piano's earliest projects and his relationship with English culture, I concentrated on Zygmunt Stanislaw Makowski after having read what he wrote in "Les Structures en plastiques de Renzo Piano" in *Plastique batiment* (February 1969). From here I recovered the initial encounters that this Polish-born engineer had with the Genoese architect Piano. Makowski's book *Steel Space Structures* (1965) has been translated into many languages and is still a reference work today, as it was for the designers of the Centre Pompidou. To understand the reasons behind the reciprocal interest that united Piano and Makowski, I found particularly helpful Makowski's essay "History of Development of Various Types of Braced Barrel Vaults and Review of Recent Achievements All Over the World," in a volume edited by Makowski, *Analysis, Design and Construction of Braced Barrel Vaults* (1985 and 2006). Piano's relationship with Makowski should be understood when considering the one Piano formed later with Robert Le Recolais, a figure key to his training and his career, as explained by L. Ciccarelli in a doctoral thesis for the University of Rome, "Piano prima di Piano: Gli anni della formazione, 1958–1971" (2015).

K. Powell is the author of three monographs dedicated to Richard Rogers that Phaidon has published since 1999, as well as a book that deals with one of the architect's most emblematic works, the headquarters of Lloyd's of London, *Lloyd's Building: Richard Rogers Partnership* (1994). I have found useful information on the life of Rogers and his work from B. Appleyard's *Richard Rogers: A Biography* (1986) and *Richard Rogers: Opere e progetti*, edited by R. Burdett (1995). As for Rogers's theoretical positions, I have made use of his own books *Architecture: A Modern View* (1990) and, with M. Fischer, *A New London* (1992).

Ove Arup & Partners and Peter Rice in particular have played roles as important as that of Piano and Rogers for the construction of the Centre Pompidou. Reading Rice's book *An Engineer Imagines* (1994) was particularly stimulating and helped me understand how Beaubourg was designed and built. In this inquiry, I relied also on the following writings of Rice, in addition to others that he wrote with colleagues from Ove Arup & Partners: "Centre Beaubourg: Introduction," *The Arup Journal* (June 2, 1973); "Main Structural Framework of the Beaubourg Centre, Paris," *Acier-Stahl-Steel* (September 1975); and "Fire Protection and Maintenance of the Centre Pompidou," *RIBA Journal* (November 1977). To learn more about the figure of Rice, I turned to the brief article by M. Pawley, "The Secret Life of the Engineers," in *Blueprint* (March 1989); the article by A. Rocca, "Peter Rice poeta del Brutalismo," in *Lotus* 78 (1993); what N. Okabe wrote *ad vocem* in Picon's *L'Art de l'ingénieur*, already mentioned; and the book (which is not always reliable) by M. Cagnoni, *Peter Rice e l'innovazione tecnica* (1996). As for the contribution of Ove Arup & Partners to the project design for the Centre Pompidou, I have espe-cially considered P. B. Ahm, F. G. Clarke, E. L. Grut, and P. Rice, "Design and Construction of the Centre National d'Art et de Culture Georges Pompidou," *Proceedings, Institution of Civil Engineers* 66 (November 1979) and 68 (August 1980).

The biography of Ove Arup that I have used, though I find the tone to be overly condescending, is that of P. Jones, *Ove Arup: Masterbuilder of the Twentieth Century* (2006), which contains a substantial bibliography. A significant part of Jones's book is dedicated to the events related to the construction of the Sydney Opera House (a fact that is all the more eloquent given the number of pages devoted to the Centre Pompidou compared to those devoted to the work of Utzon).

Ove Arup & Partners' involvement in the realization of the Sydney Opera house seemed worthy of consideration not only as it relates to the training of the engineers who participated in the construction of the Centre Pompidou but also for the intellectual mindset with which the firm confronted this project and worked with the architects. To understand this formation I wanted to further determine the ties between Buckminster Fuller and Ove Arup, although I did not succeed. To this end, among the many essays and articles devoted to the Opera House that of F. Candela, "El escándalo de la Opera de Sydney," *Arquitectura* 108 (December 1967–January 1968) struck me as one of the most convincing. In regard to the work done by Jørn Utzon in Australia, I was inspired by his writings "The Sydney Opera House," *Zodiac* 14 (1965), and "The Importance of Architects," in *Architecture in an Age of Skepticism*, edited by D. Lasdun (1984), and by the book that seemed more comprehensive, F. Fromonot, *Jørn Utzon architetto della Sydney Opera House* (1998), which contains among other things an extensive bibliography. Among the other publications I relied on are: R. Weston, *Utzon: Inspiration, Vision, Architecture* (2002); P. Murray, *The Saga of the Sydney Opera House* (2004); R. Moneo, "La costruzione dell'Opera di Sydney," in J. Utzon, *Idee di architettura: Scritti e conversazioni* (2011); and the monumental biography by P. Drew, *The Masterpiece: Jørn Utzon: A Secret Life* (2001).

For other engineers at Ove Arup & Partners involved in the Beaubourg project, I relied on the article on Frei Otto by L. Grut, T. Happold, and P. Rice in the special issue of *Architectural Design* devoted to Otto (March 1971); on the writings of T. Happold, "The Design and Construction of Diplomatic Club, Riyadh," *The Structural Engineer* 65, no. 1 (1987); "Frei Otto: The Force of Nature," *World Architecture* 8 (1990); and M. Dickson, "Frei Otto and Ted Happold, 1967 and Beyond," in *Frei Otto: Complete Works*, edited by W. Nerdinger

(2005), a comprehensive book complemented by an ample bibliography.

In the second part of the book I talk about the Centre Pompidou as an "involuntary monument." This expression derives from Alois Riegl and, in particular, from a work that I consider to be seminal: *Der moderne Denkmalkultus: Sein Wesen und seine Entstehung* (1903). In this long essay, Riegl attempted—successfully—to explain the meaning of the monument, while at the same time founding the modern concept of conservation of works of art. According to Riegl, and as cultural historian Wolfgang Kemp explains, what is true for works of art also applies to monuments. For Riegl, the concept of attention, *die Aufmerksamkeit*, is crucial in defining the value and significance of a work of art as a monument, as it relates what is considered a work or building to the person who observes it (see *Das holländische Gruppenporträt*, 1902). And it is the way in which a work or building is observed, the way in which the subject and object are related, that leads to its qualification as a monument, in the various categories defined by Reigl. Among these categories is that of the "involuntary monument," a work not designed to be a monument, but that is transformed into a monument because of how it is perceived and used. In this sense I found it legitimate in the pages of this book to speak of Beaubourg as an involuntary monument.

Acknowledgments

I would like to thank the following people for the generous assistance they provided in bringing this book to press: Nicholas Adams, Katherine Boller, Stefania Canta, Chiara Casazza, Françoise Fromonot, Shunji Ishida, Renzo Piano, Steve Piccolo, Richard Rogers, and Mirko Zardini. Each of them knows the reason for my gratitude. Some are friends going back a long way; others became so thanks to this book.

I have a special bond with Yale University. I must thank Yale University Press for the opportunity to return to Yale through the publication of this book.

The historiographic concept *contemporaneità dell'inattuale* plays an important role in the text. And for this reason, I dedicate the book to Massimo Cacciari.

Photograph Credits

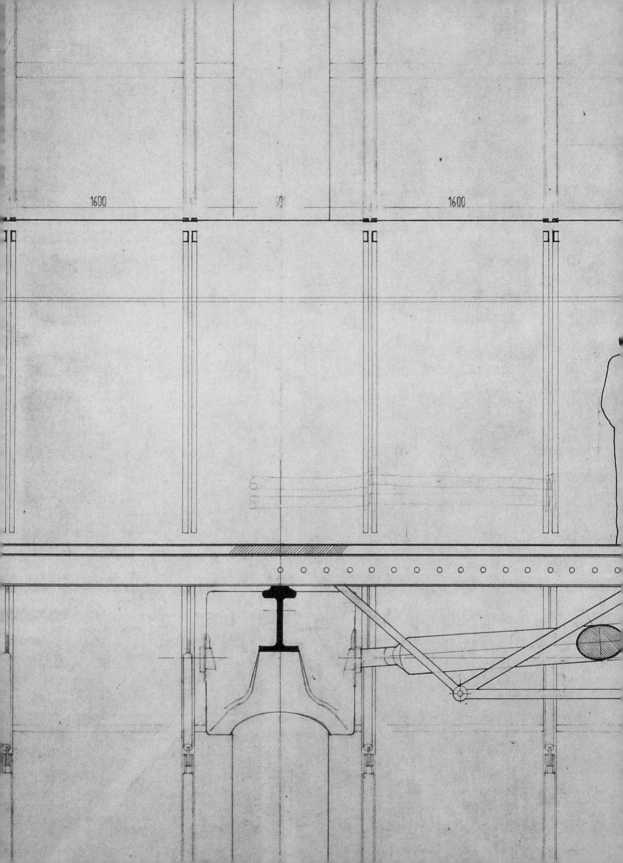

1600   50   1600

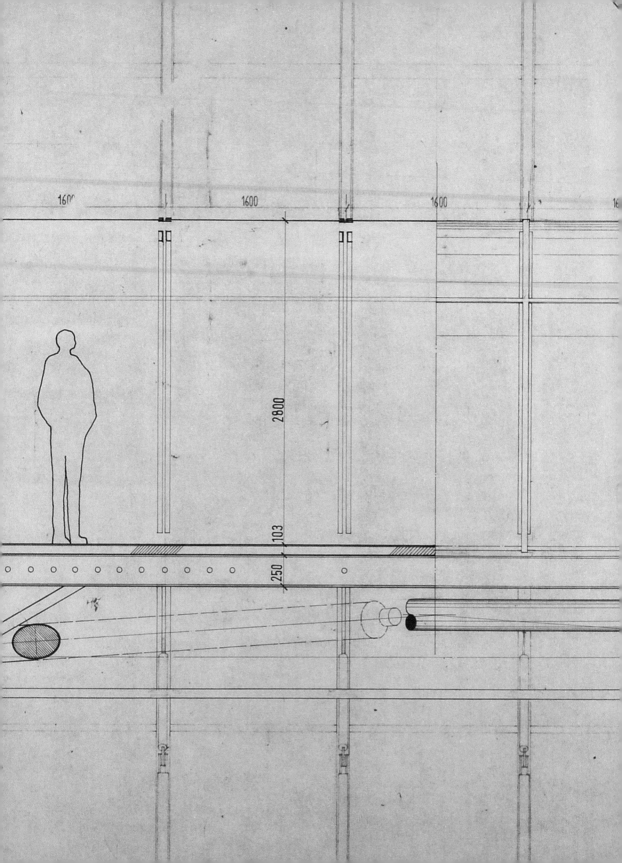